The Magic of Symbols

An introduction to symbology throughout time

HANS DIETRICH

Fair Use Disclaimer:

"The Magic of Symbols: An introduction to symbology throughout time" may contain materials such as text, images, or logos that are used for the purpose of commentary, criticism, news reporting, teaching, scholarship, or research under the principles of "fair use" as defined in copyright law. The inclusion of such materials is intended to enhance the reader's understanding and engagement with the subject matter.

The use of copyrighted material is done without seeking permission from the copyright owner, as we believe it falls within the boundaries of fair use. *"The Magic of Symbols: An introduction to symbology throughout time"* is a creative work that aims to contribute to the public discourse and provide valuable insights.

If you believe that your copyright-protected work has been used in a way that constitutes copyright infringement, please contact us at the address provided below. We will promptly address any concerns and, if necessary, make appropriate changes to ensure compliance with copyright laws.

ISBN: 979-8-9936378-2-2

Hans Dietrich

4110 SE Hawthorne Blvd. #323,

Portland OR, 97214

www.megamyst.com

"When the human race learns to read the language of symbolism, a great veil will fall from the eyes of men. They shall then know truth and, more than that, they shall realize that from the beginning truth has been in the world unrecognized, save by a small but gradually increasing number appointed by the Lords of the Dawn as ministers to the needs of human creatures struggling to regain their consciousness of divinity."

~ Manly P. Hall

A special thanks to all who supported this book especially Timothy Hogan, Grand Master of the Templar Order, OTSI Lineage, for his input and guidance around Templar symbology.

Table of Contents

A forewarning for the remainder of this book: the content herein reflects my personal research, education, interpretations, and viewpoints on the subjects under discussion.

An Introduction to Symbols, Icons, and Logos

The exploration of symbols and their dual nature as both representations of functions or ideas and as status indicators is insightful. Symbols indeed play a crucial role in our daily lives, conveying complex concepts, cultural values, and even personal or societal status. Here are a few key points about the different types of symbols from my research, understanding and opinions:

1. **Representation of Functions or Ideas:**
    - Symbols serve as characters, marks, or objects that represent functions or processes. This includes musical notes, letters representing elements in the periodic table, icons or glyphs representing complex ideas, and logos representing the essence of a company or culture.
2. **Status Symbols:**
    - Certain symbols, such as a Rolex watch, a smartphone, a fancy car, or even cosmetic surgery, serve as status symbols. These possessions indicate a person's wealth or high social and professional status. Status symbols have been sought after throughout history and can be seen in ancient burials and monumental structures.
3. **Symbology Simplifying Life's Complexities:**
    - Symbology acts as a road map that simplifies the complexities of life. It provides a guided way for individuals to navigate through ideas and concepts, allowing them to focus on their journey rather than getting bogged down by societal distractions.

4. **Deep Cultural Imprint:**
    - The understanding of symbols is ingrained in individuals from a young age, becoming a second-nature aspect encoded into their essence. Symbols help connect individuals to everyday life, cultural values, and shared knowledge.
5. **Statue of Liberty Example:**
    - The Statue of Liberty is cited as an example that holds different meanings for different people. While commonly associated with freedom, it also represents a maritime practice of liberty or authorized absence from a ship when it berths in a harbor.
    - Symbology exploration sets the stage for a deeper dive into the specific types of symbols mentioned, unraveling their hidden meanings and cultural significance. It underscores the idea that symbols are not just visual elements but carry layers of meaning and context that contribute to the rich tapestry of the human experience.
6. **Ancient Symbology Examples:**
    - Symbology is not a modern phenomenon; its roots can be traced back to the earliest reliefs of Gobekli Tepe and even further to the cave paintings of Lascaux, France. Despite being newer discoveries compared to those already known in the ancient lands of Egypt and Sumer, we are often taught that these cradles of civilization are where recognized symbology began.

Ancient Symbology

Symbology has been a part of history since the beginning of writing and drawing. We can find examples of cave art showing the symbology of hunting or anthropomorphic shamanic experiences, such as the now famous "The Sorcerer," found in the Lascaux Caves in France and dated to 13,000 BC. More modern yet still ancient examples come from Gobekli Tepe in Turkey, ancient Sumer, and, more recently, Egypt or the land of KMT (Khemit).

A depiction of anthropomorphic cave art "The Sorcerer", Lascaux France, 13,000 BC.

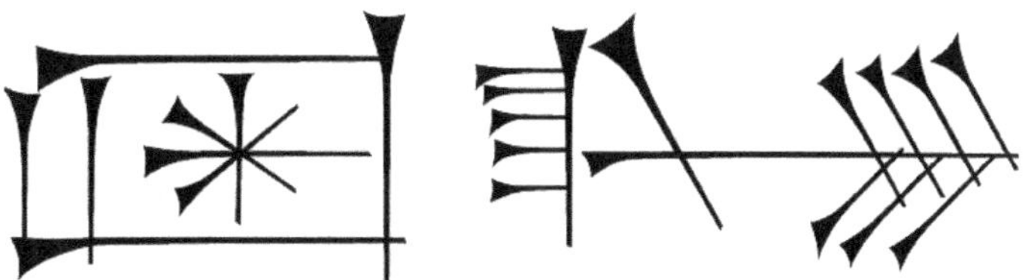

The amagi or amargi, literally meaning, "return to the mother", also associated with the word liberty as seen in the Liberty Fund logo, the first of many esoteric logos we will discuss in this book.

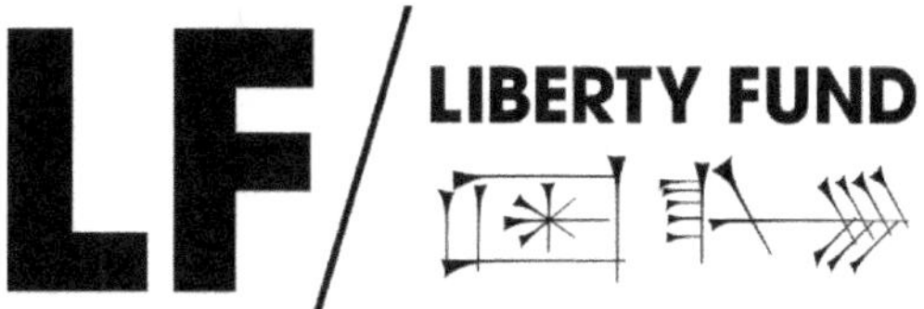

For reference, Khemitology was taught to me by my friend, scholar, and Rosicrucian Stephen Mehler, as well as Yousef Awyan and Patricia Awyan Lehman. Passed down from Yousef's father, Abd'el Hakim Awyan (Hakim), a traditions and wisdom keeper from the Awyan tribe and once a tour guide in Egypt, symbology can be found all over the ancient temples. Examples include the circle of fifths for both the houses of the land and the phases of the sun.

I touch on the five phases of the sun in the chapter on **Suns, Stars, and Sirius "Blazing Star" Symbology** later in this book; however, I will discuss the five houses here as they are equally important to discovering an alternative narrative to ancient Egyptian/Khemetian history.

To begin, it is crucial to underscore the impact of the Greek occupation of Egypt (332-30 BCE) following the conquest by Alexander the Great, which transformed the region into the Greek Ptolemaic Kingdom. This period essentially led to a rewriting of Egyptian history from the perspective of the conquerors, as history tends to be shaped by those who emerge victorious.

To clarify, pyramids were never intended as tombs; not a single "King," "Priest," or "Peasant" has ever been discovered buried within any of the ancient pyramids. In addition, there were no male Pharaohs, only Kings, however we will get into that shortly. It's important to note that in ancient Egypt, or Khemit as some prefer to call it, the Greek derivation of Egypt from the phrase "Het Ka Ptah" is significant. This phrase means the place where Ptah, the creator god and patron of Memphis, manifested in physical form (Ka). The term "Ptolemaic" is a derivation of Ptah, and as "Het Ka Ptah" evolved into "Hep Keptos," "Egyptos," and eventually "Egypt," the Greek original transliteration played a role in the origins of Coptic or Coptos. The Copts were the original Christians, referred to as the "Anointed Ones", as "Christos" roughly translates to. Similarly, the translation of Jesus to "Ye

Zeus" or the son of the Almighty, and the association with Coptos, Coptic, or Ka Ptah, the body of the almighty, unveils symbologies passed down through time but often forgotten.

The first of the five houses I learned about is called "Per Wir." This is the house of the wise, depicted by the house or broken box symbol with an elderly man under it. This is where the word "wizard" comes from and was known as a school, hospital, or university—a place of study and practice. In front of the pyramid of Djoser in Saqqara, Egypt, is a structure known as the sound hospital where sound healing occurred in the past. Sound healing is a practice used today. This site would have been known as a "Per Wir."

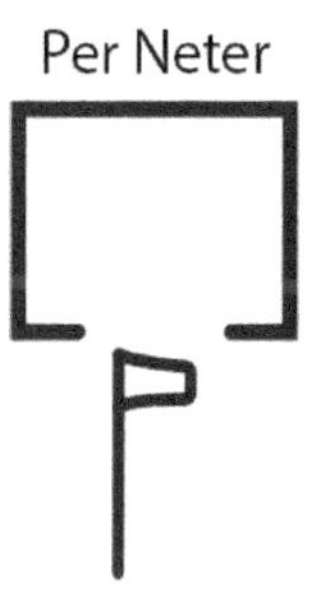

The second house was "Per Neter," the house of energy. Though the Greeks thought the neters were the gods and goddesses to the Egyptians, in fact, they represented the energies of nature. Similar deity associations are found in ancient India with the Hindu gods and goddesses and even in Central American cultures. However, Per Neter also represented the pyramid or the house of nature or energy, symbolized by the house symbol with a flag or axe under it.

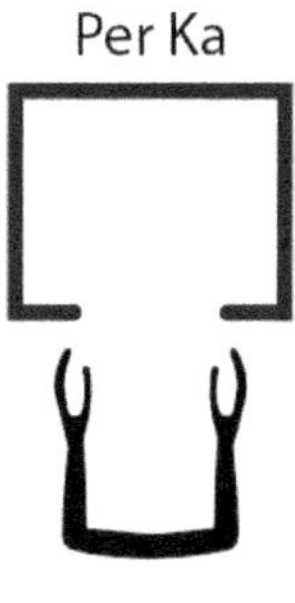

The third house was "Per Ka," the house of the body or a tomb; this is not a pyramid and is represented by the house symbol with two upraising hands representing the Ka. Similarly, the fourth house is "Per Ba," the house of spirit or worship and thus is a temple, represented by the symbol of the house with a bird's body and a man's head on it, which was the Ba—one of the seven souls to leave the

body and guide the dead to the westing lands or western lands, as the concept of death was that of following the sun to the west.

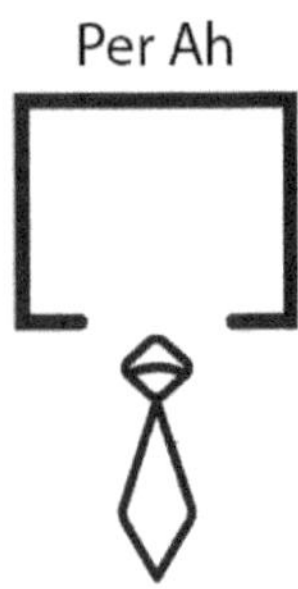

Lastly, and most importantly, is the "Per Ah," or the high house, the house of the woman. No King was crowned without the supervision and selection of the high priestesses of the temples of Isis and Hathor, and often we see in the amazing statues the woman with her arm around the man. As the society was a matriarchy or unity project, the Pharaohs or Queens ruled over the fertility of the people and the land, and the Kings oversaw the boundaries of the land and the people. Sadly, the Greeks saw this as a patrioliniage, not a matralineage, and so we are told all the Kings were Pharaohs; they were not.

King Menkaure (Mycerinus) and Queen Hathor, 2490–2472 BCE

However, a noteworthy addition is the discovery by Yousef Awyan of a sixth "per" that portrays a scene conveying the message, "From the land of Tawani (KMT), across four waters is the house of many houses." This particular "per" is known as "Per Ou," pronounced as Peru. Notably, if one follows the path of the Nile River, the Mediterranean Sea, the Atlantic Ocean, and the Amazon River, they would ultimately reach Peru. Similarly, tracing a route through the Mediterranean Sea, Red Sea, Indian Ocean, and Pacific Ocean leads to the coast of Peru. I delve into this topic further in the book, particularly in connection with the discovery of Khemitian gold artifacts labeled as Inca ceremonial burial dress wear.

There are numerous symbols to explore from the time periods of ancient Egypt/Khemit. Among those I've chosen to highlight, some feature intriguing symbolism related to the sun, as seen in depictions of Akhenaten, his wife Nefertiti, and their elongated-headed three children basking in the ultimate representation of Aten, the enlightened sun. Additionally, there is symbolism associated with water, represented by the symbol for the harmony of water, known as "Asgat Nefer." Considering that "Nefer" means harmony, it prompts a reconsideration of the name "Sneferu", recognizing it as a title. This title signifies double harmony, which is noteworthy as the Bent Pyramid in Egypt is referred to as the

Pyramid of Sneferu. It's interesting to note that the Red Pyramid is also attributed as a pyramid of Sneferu, and both structures boast two resonating internal chambers, while the Bent Pyramid uniquely features two angles of inclination in its outer layer.

Depiction of Akhenaten and his wife Nefertiti and their three daughters depicted with elongated heads bathing in the light of Aten, the Sun God symbology.

Egyptian/Khemetian hieroglyph representing the "Harmony of water" or Asgat Nefer. The foot with the jug.

Wall relief at the back side of the Temple of Isis, Philae Egypt, similar to Olmec carving of man sitting under serpent from La Venta Guatemala

Enigmatic bird man from the temple of Seti I, Abydos Egypt.

Columbia, Lucifer and The Statue of Liberty Symbology

The symbol of the Statue of Liberty is intriguing because immigrants coming to America often believed they were being granted freedom, a concept commonly associated with the Statue. However, in reality, these migrants were only granted the liberty to come ashore, not true freedom. It is noteworthy that when we observe the statue from below, we may overlook the hidden detail that it is still shackled to the podium on which it stands.

The statue has various interpretations; while some scholars and researchers perceive it as a representation of a woman or a man, it is more likely a depiction of the androgyne, reflecting the ultimate goal of the transhumanist agenda. This iconic figure symbolizes Lucifer, the light bearer, or Venus, the star of the morning. Additionally, it serves as a representation of the goddess Columbia, a symbol associated with discovery and land mass.

Christopher Columbus, although a controversial figure, was named Cristóbal de Colón, and his family seal can be found on the tomb of Pope Innocent VIII, who was suspected of being his illegitimate father. The term "Columbia" appears in various contexts, such as the South American country of Colombia, cities like Columbus, Ohio, and the District of Columbia (Washington, DC), as well as institutions like the University of Columbia and Columbine High School. References to Columbia are also seen in Hollywood, like Columbia Pictures with the Statue of Liberty as their logo, Columbia Sportswear with its directional square logo, and NASA naming the Columbia space shuttle. Additionally, the term is associated with geographical features like the Columbia Gorge and Columbia River in the Pacific Northwest of the United States. The name "Columbia" is also linked to symbolic and mythological figures, such as Isis, Ishtar, Easter, Venus, and Lucifer.

The Columbia steganography is interesting, here we have the Columbia Sportswear logo depicted as a stylized swastika or good luck symbol, also representing the "yogan" or Japanese lava motif.

Liberty shackled to the Star Fort pedestal to represent Liberty but not Freedom.

Comparison between Lucifer shackled and Columbia, the Statue of Liberty also shackled.

Lucifer depicted in the Columbia Liberty pose.

The Columbia space shuttle on re-entry, sadly this shuttle was lost in a disaster in 2003.

Columbia Pictures Liberty Columbia Goddess representation.

Esoteric Connection to the 7UP Logo

Often, I discuss the symbolism within the 7UP logo, delving into its occult and esoteric significance. For clarification, "occult" refers to hidden and magical elements and is not necessarily associated with cultist practices, as commonly assumed. Similarly, "esoteric" means intended for or likely to be understood by only a small number of people with specialized knowledge or interest. With this understanding, let's analyze the 7UP logo.

On a basic level, the 7UP logo symbolizes the 7 chakras, emanating or bubbling up from the base chakra, typically represented by a red circle. While this logo is commonly associated with a refreshing soft drink, it also serves as a metaphor for the revitalization of the chakras, ascending from the base to the crown chakra or the third eye, the pineal gland—the seat of consciousness.

Despite its association with a beverage, the logo subtly alludes to the rejuvenation of spiritual energy and awareness, starting from the foundational chakra and extending upward. The incorporation of such metaphysical concepts into advertising, particularly one targeting a broad audience, raises intriguing questions about the promotion of heightened cognitive abilities, even from a young age—a notion that may be perceived as both fascinating and, to some extent, unsettling due to its potential implications in propagandistic messaging.

Classic 7UP advertising from the 1960s

The Three Symbols

As previously mentioned, from a young age, we are introduced to three fundamental symbols: the circle, the triangle, and the square. Children's educational toys frequently incorporate these symbols as blocks that we learn to match with their corresponding holes. This early exposure serves a dual purpose, teaching us to recognize these shapes and aiding in the development of pattern recognition skills—a cognitive ability that remains with us in various forms throughout our lives.

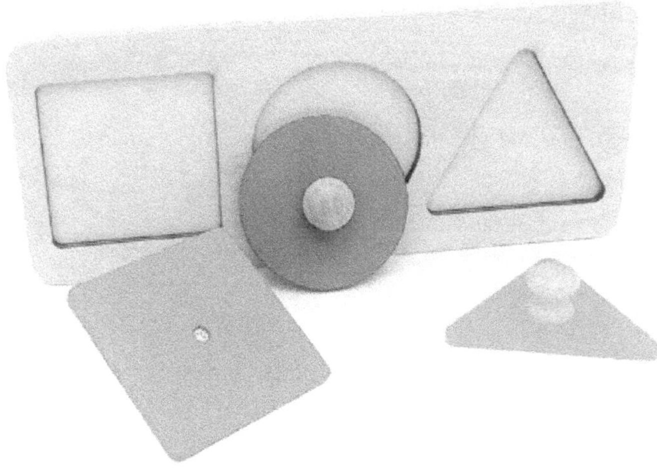

A child's game of matching the shapes of the square, the circle and the triangle.

These three shapes, the circle, triangle, and square, have a rich and ancient history. They serve as fundamental symbols reflected in various forms, including icons, logos, and objects. In ancient cultures, Zoroaster considered them as three symbols of man, particularly when stacked, embodying an anthropomorphic divinity. The founder of Aikido associated the triangle with the body, the circle with the mind, and the square with solidity.

In Zen monasteries like Kennin-ji, these three symbols, depicted as overlapping outlines in the traditional Japanese ink art known as suiboku-ga or Sumi-e, are referred to as 'the universe.' This artistic representation reflects a philosophical and physical concept, suggesting that the combination of these three forms within a cylinder leads to oneness.

Zen depiction of the three symbols representing the Universe.

"Man is symbolized by three elements, one on top of another: circle—triangle—square."

~ Zoroaster

•••

"The principle of 'Sanmi–Sangen' explains the mystery of life. Sanmi–Sangen means the three elements that constitute the basis of all forms of existence. These basic symbols both explain the meaning of and guide the destiny of human life."

~ Yukitaka Yamamoto

•••

"The body should be triangular, the mind circular. The triangle represents the generation of energy and is the most stable physical posture. The circle symbolizes serenity and perfection, the source of unlimited techniques. The square stands for solidity, the basis of applied control."

~ Ueshiba Morihei, founder of aikido

During my time at Art School from 1995 to 1998, one of the initial graphic design classes delved into the concept of positive and negative spatial representations through black and white shapes. This concept is reminiscent of the symbolism found in Yin and Yang.

Classic Yin and Yang symbology. Yin is negative, dark, and feminine, Yang positive, bright, and masculine. Their interaction is thought to maintain the harmony of the universe and to influence everything within it.

In my graphic design classes, we were also introduced to the three design principles: the circle, triangle, and square. These shapes, either individually or in combination, served as the foundational elements for various designs, symbols, and logos. However, the magical and alchemical aspects of these shapes were not initially emphasized in my education.

I prefer to refer to these as the Three Magical Symbols, and their magical nature stems from the intrinsic qualities of the symbols themselves. Before the advent of modern graphic design software like Adobe® Photoshop®, Adobe® Illustrator®, or even CoralDRAW®, design students, including myself, were instructed to use tools akin to those employed by Master Masons to craft these shapes.

Creating the Circle, Triangle and Square

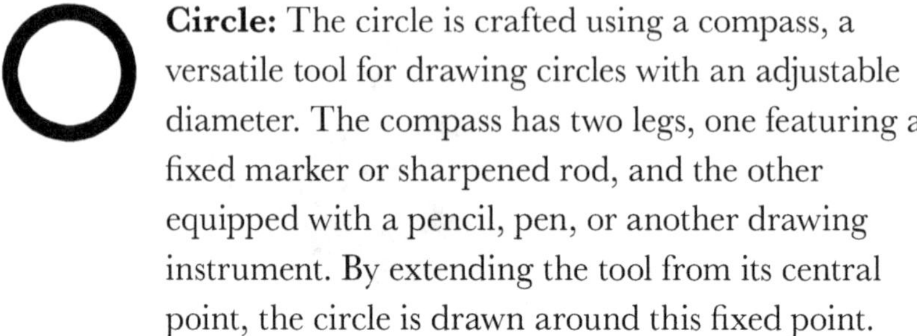

Circle: The circle is crafted using a compass, a versatile tool for drawing circles with an adjustable diameter. The compass has two legs, one featuring a fixed marker or sharpened rod, and the other equipped with a pencil, pen, or another drawing instrument. By extending the tool from its central point, the circle is drawn around this fixed point.

Triangle: The triangle is formed using a straight edge or square rule in conjunction with the compass. The compass aids in locating the triangle's points, after which the straight edge or square rule is employed to connect these points, resulting in the formation of a triangle.

Square: The square is generated by using the compass to identify the four corners, alongside the square rule and a general ruler to draw the lines constituting the sides of the square.

A depiction of a traditional compass tool with a squared straight edge, the overall symbol of Free Masons.

All these tools have been employed by master masons not only in the construction of great structures worldwide but also in navigating the oceans. While the magnetic compass aids in finding direction, the drafter's compass is utilized to measure distances on a map, which is then correlated with the ruler or squared rule to navigate both longitude and latitude on a map.

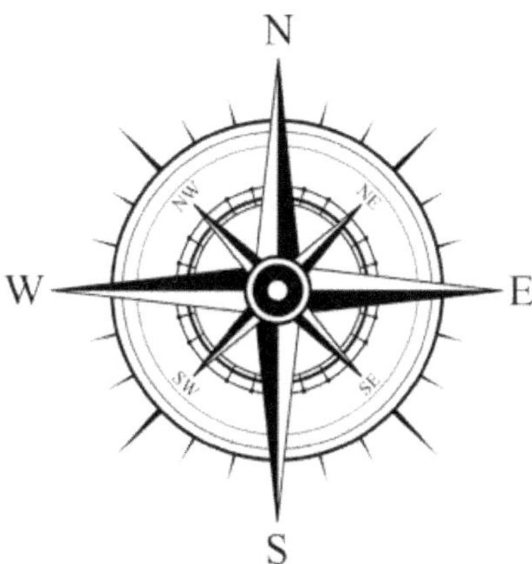

The 8 directions of the compass points.

As mentioned earlier, these three shapes can be identified in various forms in almost every symbol, icon, or logo. In a 3D rendering environment, the triangle serves as a polymorphic shape or polygonal mesh that covers a 3D object, providing it with artificial dimensionality. Depending on the size of the polygons, realistic colors, lighting, shadows, and environments can be captured. Although there might still be an uncanny valley effect to the viewer, as our eyes see in rods and cones (or circles and triangles) and cannot perceive detail beyond about 200 dpi (dots per inch), our eyes and perception often blend details together.

In a transcendental state of consciousness, this effect is exaggerated, and individuals may witness polygraphic shapes with vivid colors. The barriers of perceived realities are torn down, replaced with strobing movements, stunning geometry, and often what is referred to as the “machine elves.” This, however, is a topic to be discussed later, as mankind has undoubtedly drawn symbols from this altered state or realm of existence, as seen in psychedelic art and even the mathematical fractal geometry found in science and nature.

The Three Magical Symbols

However, let’s return to why these are considered magical symbols. I refer to them as such because they have various representations, and “multipliers” can be added to them to imbue them with more profound purpose and esoteric understanding.

For example, we can consider the simplicity of the circle, the triangle, and the square, focusing primarily on the gematria or the assignment of numbers to them. The circle represents 1 since it has only one side. The triangle represents 3 as it has 3 sides, and the square represents 4 because it has 4 sides.

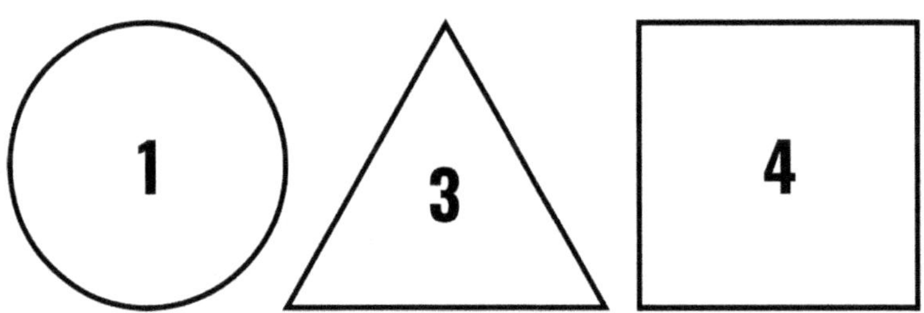

Adding 1+3+4 gives us the number 8, which is undeniably a magical number. Eight represents the number of fingers we have on our hands, excluding the thumbs. There are 8 sides to a stop sign, and there are 8 cardinal directions—N, S, E, W, as well as NW, NE, SW, SE. It’s intriguing that the standard 4 cardinal points form an anagram for NEWS and so forth. The number 8 is also often associated with prosperity and money, but it is equally linked to concepts such as infinity, spiritual perfection, completeness, and purity, rendering it a divine number.

Businesses in the know may associate client bills with numbers that add up to 8, aiming to cast a spell on the project's outcome, signifying completion and purity. This number is also one less than 9, which is the number of the magician and symbolizes god-like attributes. While we will delve into the symbology of the number 9 later, let's refocus on the three shapes.

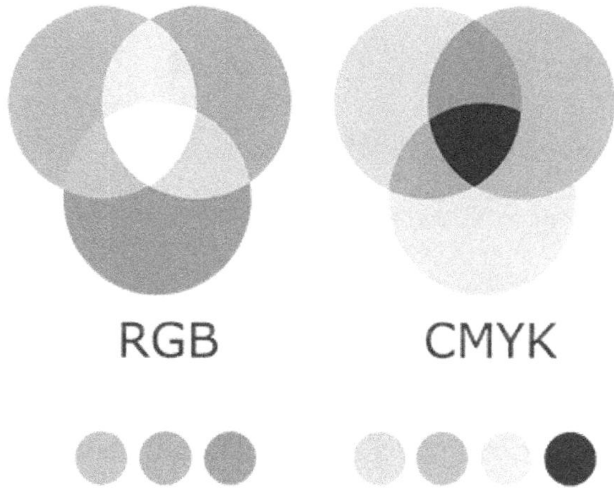

Depiction of the light and pigment color charts.

If we fill in the outlines of the three shapes, we can assign colors as the next multiplier. The circle becomes blue, the triangle becomes red, and the square becomes green. In color theory, these are the colors of light. Combining red, green, and blue lights, known to designers as RGB, creates a "white magical light." When you combine RGB as color pigments, you get the color "rich black," as seen in the CMYK example. RGB (red, green, blue) is always associated with mixing colors of light, while CMYK (cyan, magenta, yellow, black) is associated with pigment colors. This makes both approaches alchemical in nature, as in alchemy, we attempt to transform the prima materia or primitive form of matter, regolith, or dirt through a process of combining it with distilled water and plasma fire to create an element of light or purity—the philosopher's stone. This process evolves from rich black to dark red and eventually concludes as a white powder of monoatomic elements. This takes us to the next multiplier for these shapes, which is elements.

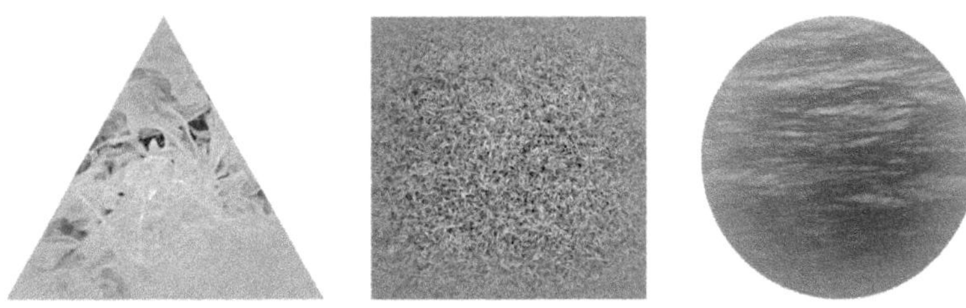

The fire triangle, the earth square and the water circle.

By assigning elements to the three shapes and incorporating colors, we create the circle as blue, representing water. The triangle becomes red, symbolizing fire. Lastly, the square becomes green, signifying earth or vegetation. Thus, by burning the earth through the combination of water and fire, we initiate the alchemical process of transformation, leading to the creation of the philosopher's stone, symbolizing prosperity, immortality, or monoatomic elements of earth born from the fire. In essence, man is a process encompassing all of this.

Taking the multipliers one step further, we can assign dimensionality to each. The blue, water circle becomes the sphere, representing the watery planet we live on. The red, fire triangle becomes the tetrahedron, a 4-sided pyramid, where, in Greek symbolism, the pyramid represents the fire from within. Lastly, the green, earth square becomes the cube, a 6-sided representation of the earth and our 6 continents: North America, South America, Europe, Asia, Africa, and Antarctica.

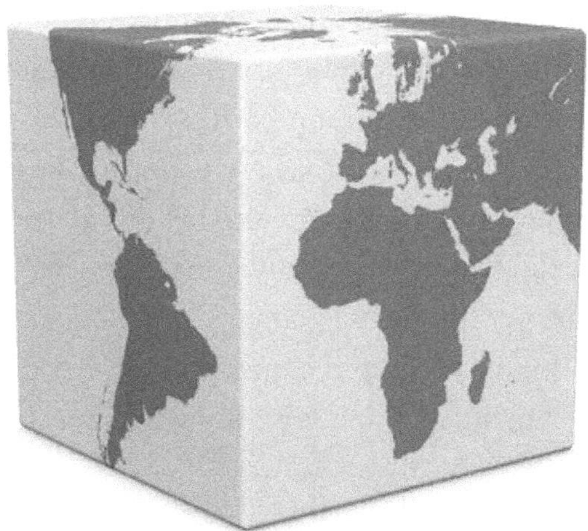

Depiction of the earth cube.

It is fascinating to note that these dimensional shapes are ubiquitous, frequently appearing in corporate logos and occult or hidden symbology. These shapes exert subtle influences on our daily lives, yet often go unnoticed. This symbological approach to society has a rich history, dating back thousands of years, evident in both Sumerian and Egyptian glyphs and art.

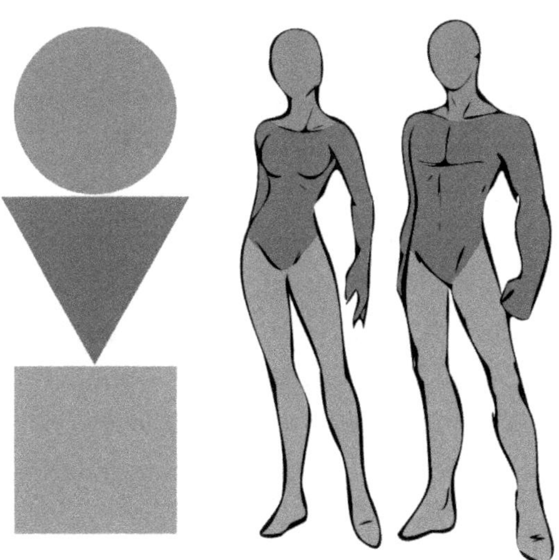

Depiction of the human (hue man = colored man).

The final phase of adding multipliers to these three shapes

involves stacking them in a manner reminiscent of their Zoroastrian history as the symbols of man. The water sphere represents the head of the human body, symbolizing water due to its connection with the head, where water intake occurs to fuel and lubricate the rest of the body. The head is a crucial hub for various bodily fluids, including saliva, tears, mucus, sweat, and the sacred waters of the pineal gland. The pineal gland produces DMT during dream states and death, while the brain synthesizes substances like amrita or soma, also known as melatonin, regulating sleep and healing.

Adding the torso or the inverted tetrahedron, representing the fire element, encompasses the body's dynamic processes. This region houses vital functions such as the pumping of the heart, circulation of lifeblood, digestion of food into fuel, and conversion of breath chemicals in the lungs to regulate body temperature. It also includes organs like the liver and kidneys, as well as the sacred womb in women, where new generations are conceived. This area is the alchemical crucible of the body, breaking down fuel into the light and fuels of life.

These two shapes stack on top of the green earth cube, symbolizing the lush fertility of life. The earth cube is linked to the cycle of life and death, decomposition, fertilization, and rebirth. Excrement, in the form of urine and feces, is a vital part of this cycle. In men, life-giving sperm is found in the lower torso, acting as a fertilizer that injects new life into the upper torso by inseminating an egg. The lower torso also connects us to the earth through our feet, symbolizing a profound connection with the planet's energies, especially in times when people were barefoot.

Through these multipliers, we gain insights into the divinity of our human makeup, revealing the magical essence of who we are.

Circle, Triangle and Square: The Base Shapes for Other Design Elements

Circles serve as the foundation for spirals, spheres, and globes, often symbolizing planets and moons.

Squares transform into cubes, chevrons, arrows, or boxes, providing containment.

Triangles manifest as pyramids, tetrahedrons, and abstract forms like stars, Merkabah, and other sacred geometric shapes.

Consequently, these three shapes and their multipliers serve as fundamental elements for numerous symbols and logos.

Throughout history, various attributes have been assigned to these shapes. For example, the square is linked to the Sun God, the circle to the Moon God, and the triangle to the God of the Stars. These enduring shapes of power are ingrained in the basics of life and design.

Additionally, each of these shapes carries secondary attributes and associated symbols.

Stars:

There are numerous representations of stars, ranging from multi-pointed stars to symbols associated with the sun. Three-dimensional stars, such as the Merkabah, and intricate flower-like shapes like the 64-star tetrahedron, contribute to the rich variety of star symbology.

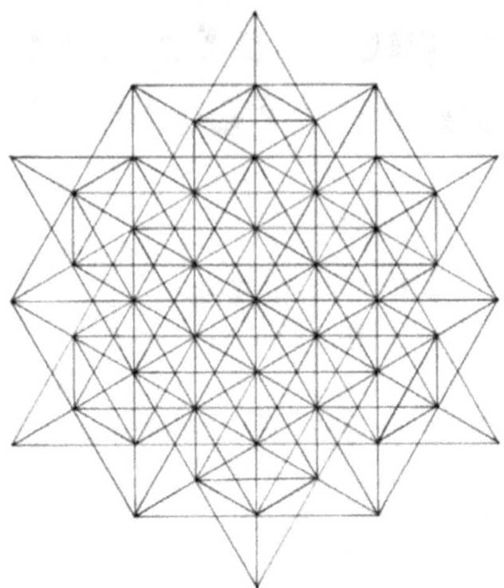

The 64-star tetrahedron.

The Cross:

The square, representing grounding, combined with a reach towards the divine, creates a meaningful symbol. When tilted, it can also signify the X, holding an intriguing aspect of steganography. This symbol has ties to the Vitruvian man, as seen in Da Vinci's renowned depiction, with feet firmly planted and hands outstretched. The X can also symbolize a division of realities, serving as a portal to other dimensions. This shape is echoed in the Inca cross or Chakana, prominent in indigenous American art, depicting the steps of the past, present, and future, along with the sun within the sun. Additionally, unfolding the six sides of a cube results in the formation of the cross shape.

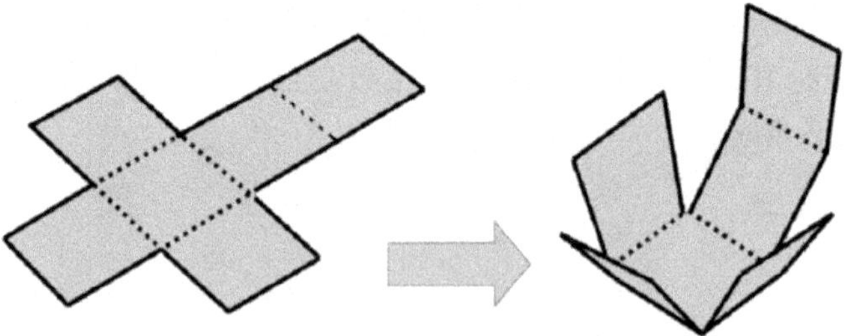

The unfolded cube makes the cross.

Serpents:

The snake frequently symbolizes kundalini energy or physical healing, often depicted as an S-shape, a snake, or even a dragon or lizard when viewed with an open perspective. In the Garden of Eden, the serpent is associated with temptation. The caduceus also incorporates a snake within its triadic symbolism, representing the thrice-great Hermes.

The Caduceus, a Harold's wand, with wings and wrapped with the 2 serpents of DNA.

Animals:

Eagles, dragons, and lions emerge as three of the most employed animal symbols throughout ancient to modern times. Their depictions adorn royal crests, territorial flags, and protective monuments worldwide, with one of the oldest and notable examples being the two-headed eagle.

The double headed eagle of the Romans, Germans, and the United States.

Wings:

The bird, owl, butterfly are a good example of winged used of this symbol. We also find angels and demons with wings, and even ancient Gods and Goddesses, like the Goddess Isis is depicted with wings.

The winged goddess Isis from ancient Egypt/Khemit.

Trees:

The depiction of trees often carries profound symbolic meaning, commonly associated with the Tree of Knowledge in the Garden of Eden. However, trees can also represent the Tree of Life, a symbol found in various cultures, including the Kabbalah with its sacred depiction known as the Tree of Sephiroth or Tree of Life symbology.

In the Garden of Eden narrative, the tree symbolizes the source of knowledge and the moral choice between good and evil. The tree's fruit, often depicted as an apple, is forbidden to Adam and Eve, leading to consequences for disobeying divine orders.

Alternatively, the Tree of Life is a universal symbol present in diverse spiritual and cultural contexts. In Kabbalah, an esoteric tradition within Judaism, the Tree of Sephiroth represents the divine structure of creation. It consists of ten interconnected spheres, or Sephiroth, each symbolizing a different aspect of existence and divinity.

Beyond religious contexts, trees symbolize growth, connection, and the cycles of life. Their roots delve deep into the earth, grounding them, while branches reach toward the heavens, embodying a link between the earthly and the divine. The symbolism of trees as embodiments of life, knowledge, and spirituality resonates across cultures and throughout human history.

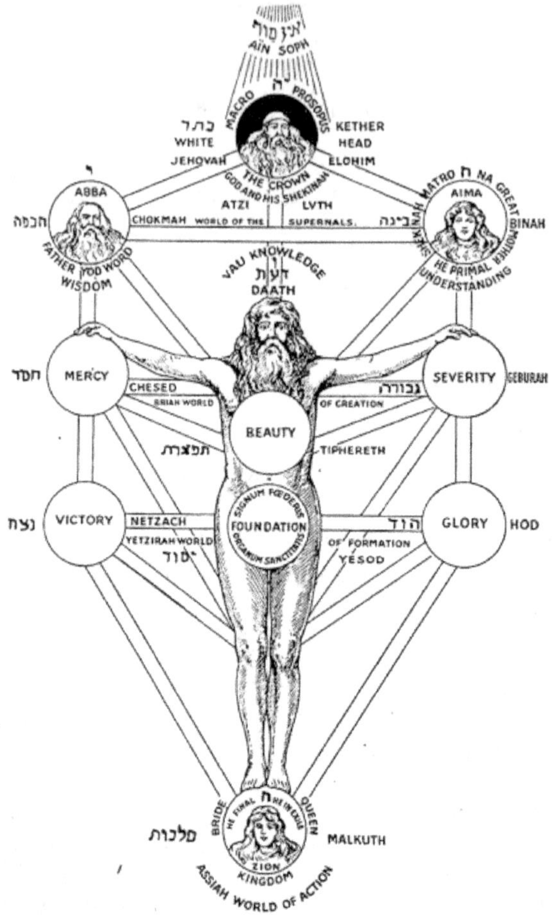

THE SACRED TREE OF THE SEPHIROTH

The sacred tree of the Sephiroth representing the 33 different paths and places.

Tools:

Tools serve as potent symbols, embodying ancient Masonic magic and conveying mysterious teachings from times past. Each tool carries unique symbolism, often associated with specific virtues, values, or aspects of human endeavor. Some notable tools and their symbolic meanings include:

1. **Hammer:** Symbolizes force, creation, and strength. In the context of Masonic symbolism, it represents the constructive force that shapes and molds reality.

2. **Compass and Square:** Embody the principles of morality and virtue. The compass signifies a tool for circumscribing desires and keeping within due bounds, while the square represents morality and virtue.

3. **Ruler:** Represents precision, order, and measurement. In symbolic terms, it signifies the importance of adhering to ethical standards and principles.

4. **Plow and Sickle:** These agricultural tools symbolize labor, abundance, and the cycle of life. They are often associated with the fruitful harvest resulting from diligent work.

5. **Turbine and Mill:** Represent industry, innovation, and technological progress. These tools symbolize the transformative power of human ingenuity and the evolution of society.

6. **Keys:** Symbolize access, knowledge, and authority. Keys are often associated with unlocking hidden or sacred knowledge and represent the stewardship of important information.

7. **Shields:** Signify protection, defense, and strength. Shields are emblematic of safeguarding oneself or others from external threats.

8. **Arrowheads and Bullets:** Symbolize focus, precision, and the potential for both constructive and destructive forces. They represent the impact and consequences of directed energy.

The hammer and sickle, gained prominence as a symbol of communist unity, emphasizing the collaboration between the working class (represented by the hammer) and the peasantry (represented by the sickle). This iconic symbol is associated with socialism and the pursuit of a classless society.

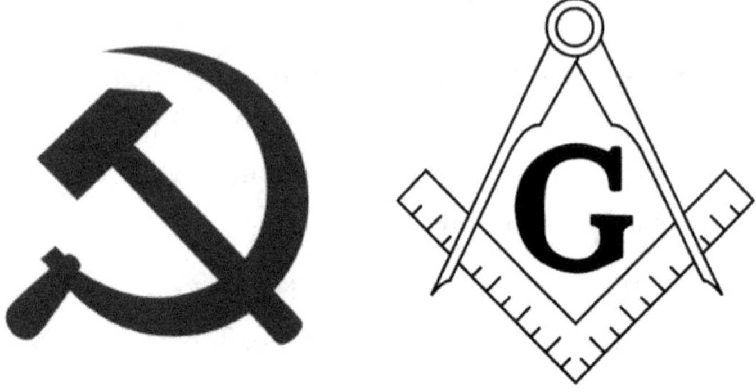

The Soviet hammer and sickle and the Compass, Square and G (God, Geometry, Gnosis) of the Masons.

These tools and their symbolic meanings have resonated throughout history, carrying diverse interpretations across different cultures and belief systems. They serve as a rich tapestry of human understanding and aspiration, encapsulating the essence of various trades, virtues, and ideologies.

Architecture:

Symbols such as cathedrals, buildings, columns, checkered floors, stained glass, and historical monuments like obelisks and pyramids are laden with rich symbolism, often carrying deep cultural, spiritual, or esoteric meanings. Here's a brief exploration of some of these symbols:

1. **Cathedrals and Buildings:**
    - **Architecture:** The design and layout of cathedrals and other buildings often incorporate sacred geometry, which is believed to have spiritual significance. The use of arches, domes, and spires may symbolize ascent toward the divine.

2. **Columns:**
   - **Strength and Support:** Columns are not only architectural elements but also symbols of strength and support. In classical architecture, columns are often associated with specific orders (Doric, Ionic, Corinthian), each carrying its own symbolic attributes.
3. **Checkered Floors:**
   - **Duality:** Checkered floors, commonly seen in Masonic symbolism, represent the dual nature of existence — the interplay of light and dark, good and evil, or spiritual and material aspects of life.
4. **Stained Glass:**
   - **Divine Light:** Stained glass windows in religious structures are designed to filter and project light, symbolizing divine illumination. The colorful scenes often depict religious narratives or saints.
5. **Obelisks:**
   - **Phallic Symbolism:** Obelisks, with their tall, slender form, are often associated with phallic symbolism. In ancient Egypt, they were erected as monuments to gods or prominent individuals.
6. **Pyramids:**
   - **Cosmic Symbolism:** Pyramids, especially in ancient Egypt, symbolize the cosmic journey of the soul. The structure's shape represents the rays of the sun converging at a central point, reflecting spiritual ascent.

These symbols, when examined within specific cultural, religious, or philosophical contexts, reveal layers of meaning that go beyond their physical forms. Additionally, some symbols, like the checkered floor in Masonic lodges, are intentionally veiled in mystery, meant to convey esoteric teachings to initiates.

It's crucial to approach the interpretation of these symbols with an understanding of the cultural and historical contexts in which they originated. They continue to be subjects of study, contemplation, and fascination, offering glimpses into the collective human quest for meaning and connection with the divine.

6 of the 9 pyramids of Giza, the 3 larger pyramids reflecting the belt stars of Orion/Osiris.

There are even uses of the three shapes hidden in our daily lives and representing the hidden multipliers through interpretation.

Circle, Triangle and Square Hidden in Plain Sight

In my research I have noticed the symbolism of the circle, triangle and square to be the key controls and components identified in TV and video remote controls. This interesting discovery suggests a connection between elemental symbolism and the functions of the buttons. Here's a breakdown:

1. **Triangle (Fire Element):**
   - **Function:** "Play" or "Start"
   - **Symbolic Interpretation:** Represents the lighting of the fire of entertainment, initiating the action.
2. **Square (Earth Element):**
   - **Function:** "Stop"
   - **Symbolic Interpretation:** Grounds the process or the forward movement of entertainment, bringing it to a halt.
3. **Broken Square:**
   - **Function:** "Pause"
   - **Symbolic Interpretation:** Indicates a temporary pause in the process, suggesting that it can resume.
4. **Two Triangles (Fire Element):**
   - **Functions:** "Fast Forward" and "Fast Rewind"
   - **Symbolic Interpretation:** Guides the fire, speeding up or slowing down the entertainment process.

5. **Circle (Water Element):**
    - **Function:** "Record"
    - **Symbolic Interpretation:** Represents the retention of memory, akin to recording.
6. **Central Directional Button System:**
    - **Function:** "Navigate the Menu"
    - **Symbolic Interpretation:** Resembles the facets of a crystal or star, offering various directions and options, much like navigating through menu items.

The use of elemental symbolism in everyday objects, even in technology like remote controls, adds an intriguing layer to our interactions with these devices. It reflects how symbols and archetypes persist in modern culture, often subconsciously influencing our perceptions and experiences.

Moreover, the incorporation of elemental symbolism in gaming controllers, such as the Triangle, Square, Circle, and X buttons, further highlights the pervasive nature of these symbols across various technological interfaces. This blending of ancient symbolic concepts with contemporary technology demonstrates the enduring power of archetypal imagery in shaping our understanding of the world around us.

Live In Y○ur W×rld, Pl△y In □urs.

Play Station symbolism using the circle, triangle and square.

Interestingly we also find these symbols on the characters found in the popular Korean TV show, Squid Games.

Characters from the popular Korean TV show, the Squid Games, using the circle, triangle, and square symbology.

My interpretation of the On/Off/Power button as creating an instant wireless "star-gate/wormhole" of data between the remote or gaming control device and audio/video/gaming devices adds a fascinating layer of symbolism to this ubiquitous feature. Here's a breakdown of this analysis:

On/Off/Power Button:

- **Symbolism:** Represents the initiation and cessation of power or energy flow.
- **Function:** Creates an instant wireless connection, acting as a metaphorical "star-gate" or "wormhole" for data transmission.

Symbolic Interpretation:

- **Initiation of Power:** When pressed "On," it symbolizes the activation of energy or power, transforming the device from a dormant state to an active one.
- **Cessation of Power:** When pressed "Off," it symbolizes the deactivation or cessation of energy flow, returning the device to a dormant state.

Metaphorical Reference:

- **Star-Gate/Wormhole:** Describes the rapid and seamless transfer of data, drawing a metaphorical parallel to the instantaneous travel through a star-gate or wormhole.

Connection to Wormhole Technology:

- **Laboratory-Level Technology:** Highlights the existence of wormhole technology at a laboratory, bench level.
- **Overlooked Aspect:** Emphasizes that this technological capability is often overlooked or missed, perhaps due to its routine integration into everyday devices.

This perspective draws attention to the symbolic and metaphorical aspects of technology, showing how even seemingly mundane features like power buttons can be imbued with deeper meanings. Additionally, it prompts contemplation on the advanced technologies that we encounter daily and may not fully appreciate or understand in their intricate details.

Symbols found in Logos and Brand:

A Select Few Circular Logos

Apple:

Not traditionally thought of as a water element, or a circle, the apple is rounded and juicy and has an "original sin" bite mark removed from it which symbolically becomes the leaf, using the entire shape of the rounded apple.

Of note: The original Apple logo was newton sitting under the apple tree symbolizing the spark of creativity, but also the garden of Eden moment when a bite is taken from the fruit of the tree of knowledge.

ATT:

A blue water globe with clouds, also represents fiber optics or fluid technology of the American Telephone and Telegraph company. There are also 11 stripes which represent a master number, the spiritual messenger, and the also the number of disorder and the 11th hour.

Of note: it is interesting that 11, 22, 33, etc. are considered master numbers, 11 represents the 2 pillars of freemasonry, which symbolically fell on 9/11. 22 is the number of Mary Magdalene who holds the sacred blood line, and 33 is the highest ranking in Free Masonry.

European Space Agency - ESA:

The ESA logo represents the earth with the placement of the "e", and our moon with the dot, while surrounded by space. As Earth is primarily a water-based planet, the negative space in the e could also represent an ocean and the ligature of the e a continent, perhaps Europe.

Of note: The dot could also represent the space station, or even the star of Sirius which would represent the future, which all space missions are a representation of.

HP Hewlett Packard:

Another circular or spherical water bases logo is HP which as of recent was a circular blue logo with the letters H and P occupying the negative or inverted space of the circle. This of course stands for Hewlett and Packard, the founders of the company, but in a subtle more occult reference refers to human potential and hierarchy and purpose.

Of note: Although the monogram of HP in the circle represents the names of the founders of the company in 1939, it is intriguing that Cosmicism and occult writer HP Lovecraft died in 1937 and the HP could also be a nod to his writings and work.

A Select Few Triangle Logos

Adidas:

When we look at triangular or pyramidical logos we can see the logo for ADIDAS which is a 3-tiered pyramid and represents a stylized A, or the steps of success, and even the 3 tiers of sport awards with bronze or copper, silver, and gold.

Of note: The name Adidas comes from the founder of the company Adolf Dassler which shortened becomes Adidas.

Delta:

This airline logo is a pyramid design showing 2 sides of the pyramid, colored in our color theory fire red. In Greek pyramid means fire within. Planes carry fuel and thus burn that fuel to fly.

The pyramid is broken by a chevron of blank space showing both lift and directional or wave movement.

Of Note: Delta waves occur in the brain, when one is in the deepest state of relaxation and deep sleep, and delta also represents many streams of water flowing into one.

Ethereum:

This crypto currency logo is in the shape of a transparent octahedron or 2 flipped pyramids, with the dark portions being the bottom of the upper pyramid shape or the same for the flipped pyramid below. Interesting that this also appears like a polygon eye like the diamond shape of a Chameleon's eye seen from head on.

Of note: it is interesting that the Ethereum currency is decentralized, but their logo is very centrally focused.

America Online – AOL:

The AOL logo has changed a bit over the years, originally it was a triangle with a vortex spinning inside, representing the fire within. However, if you look closely the vortex and triangle combination does subtly and spell out AOL, a pareidolia or trickery of sight of sorts, seeing something in a shape that may not actually be there.

Of note: Now, however, in the new AOL logo, the triangle has been rotated to face right, thus showing movement forward.

A Select Few Cube and Square Logos

Microsoft:

Microsoft is a familiar logo always displaying its 4 colored boxes. This is symbolic of their main product which was Windows and is represented with the stain glass "window" colors of red, green, blue, and gold or "light". Microsoft also has their new product Microsoft 365, which uses a stylistic cube or hexagon in movement for its logo or mark. This is similar to the rotating hexagonal storm we see most prominent at the north pole of Saturn. Most cube and square symbology have a Saturnian root within.

Of note: It interesting when breaking apart meaning of micro, small, and soft which could mean soft and cuddly or approachable but is also a shortening for software, while the stain glass windows represent vision, reflection and even the windows to our soul, our eyes.

Nintendo Game Cube:

This logo is designed as a cube within a cube; however, it also represents the path of a labyrinth or game. If we look closely at the shape of the colored gradient connected boxes, it creates the shape of the "G "and the negative space in-between makes up the shape of the "C".

Of note: The hexagon and the cube are both shapes that represent Saturn, and in this case, it looks as if there is a ring around the central cube visually expressing Saturn.

Rubik's Cube:

The Rubik's logo has always fascinated me, not so much the blocky logotype, which almost acts as a distraction from the true gold of this logo, the cube itself. There are 54 colored faces on the surface of the cube separated into groups of 9 faces and 6 colors. 54 in gematria is 5+4 which is nine. The sides of the cube are showing, which is 27 faces separated into groups of 9 faces and 3 colors showing. In gematria 27 is 2+7 which also is nine. If you look at the logo as a box, it is radiating golden light. The 3 colors showing are blue, red and gold.

Of note: If you look at the cube as an extension of the earth element, and thus land to be ruled over. The objective of the puzzle is to organize all 9 faces of a single color onto one of the 6 sides of the cube, which like war, is a calculated strategy of organizing people and land.

A Select Few Star-Based Logos

CenturyLink:

This logo is interesting, it's a star like circle with triangular elements and earth colors from our color theory example earlier. There is also the though symbology also represents green technology. Hidden in the logo are six light green, and six dark green triangles, and six intersecting lines, creating a subliminal 666 hidden within.

Of note: This could be a reference to Venus or Lucifer the fallen angel, as green is also the color of envy and Lucifer also fell to Earth.

Sirius:

The Sirius logo says it all, it shows a nebulous "S" with the blazing star of Sirius as the negative space intersecting all sides of the S. Sirius is a Star system that has roots in almost every religion and culture around the planet at one time or another, and currently is the Blazing Star of the Masonic orders and represents the perfect man as well as the origin of the original lodge.

Of note: Sirius is also known as the Dog star and appears in the sky around the dog days of summer, so it is interesting that the Sirius Satellite Radio logo is a black dog, who's eye is Sirius, representing the dog star and space. The black dog is like the Tiangou in Chinese legend and the Wolf Star in Tibetan lore.

On Star:

Another possible reference to the Blazing Star of Sirius, or Venus on the horizon is the On Star logo. The logo is also in the shape of an "on" button, giving a representation to turning the product on and it being a star feature.

Of note: In the ancient languages of Khemitian and Phoenician, the word "On" meant bright, so in this case the logo subtly translates to Bright Star, a nod to those in the know.

Combination Symbols using the Circle, Triangle, and Square

The Deathly Hallows and the Philosopher's Stone of Alchemy:

For Harry Potter enthusiasts, the Deathly Hallows symbol, consisting of a triangle, circle, and line (resembling a square), symbolizes key elements: the triangle stands for the invisibility cloak, the circle represents the resurrection stone, and the line, akin to a square, signifies the formidable Elder Wand. Notably, this symbol shares a remarkable resemblance with the one linked to the Philosopher's Stone in alchemy.

Of note: wizards and druids in the old times made their magic wands out of holly wood, as holly has alchemical properties. The wand was said to be able to cast magical spells often bedazzling those it was used on with a silver light. Today we go to the movie theaters to watch the magic of Hollywood bedazzle us with light upon the silver screen.

The Ankh:

The ankh, often hailed as the key of life, stands out as a captivating amalgamation of symbols, incorporating the elements of a triangle, a square, and a circle, or in this particular context, a tear drop. Intriguingly, this symbol has undergone a transformation in contemporary times, where it has come to embody the essence of womanhood through the symbol of the female.

Of note: the ankh carries profound significance, extending beyond its conventional interpretations. In addition to being a timeless symbol, it is believed to represent the sacred womb space within a woman. In this symbolic framework, the vaginal canal is equated with the square or rectangle, the uterus assumes the form of the tear drop-shaped circular element, while the fallopian tubes and ovaries are attributed to the triangular components of the ankh. This nuanced interpretation unveils the symbol's association with the divine aspects of femininity and the reproductive process, offering a rich tapestry of meaning that transcends its historical roots. The ankh, thus, becomes a powerful emblem not only of life but also of the intricate and divine nature of the feminine experience.

Esoteric Symbolism Found in Movies

In my Dropa Legends & Lore book, I addressed how many esoteric ideas come across in movies, especially in the Star Wars saga. I feel I need to address some of this symbolism in this book as well, as it is dedicated to uncovering occult and esoteric symbolism missed in daily life. Although Star Wars is a great start and probably one of the most esoterically symbolic movie franchises of our times, there are others for sure. But let's begin here, with the Star Wars Saga.

Outside of my exploration into Merkabah technology found in Star Wars with Darth Vader's meditation chamber as depicted. We also have the astral projection aspects found in "Star Wars: The Last Jedi" (2017), as well as the light body knowledge portrayed in the original saga, Episodes 4, 5, and 6, with Obi Wan and Yoda becoming light beings to help Luke. This also occurs in "Star Wars: The Rise of Skywalker" (2019), but there are other esoteric knowledge key points found in these movies.

Darth Vader's meditation chamber as depicted in "Star Wars: The Empire Strikes Back" (1980).

For instance, the torture, the crucifixion, and thus the resurrection of Han Solo become eminent in "Star Wars: The Empire Strikes Back" (1980) when Han Solo (Solo is a reference to being alone but also has ties to the troublemaker in the Jesus Christ consciousness and thus character) is captured by Darth Vader on Bespin, the Cloud City. He is tortured for information before he is thrown into the pit to be encased in Carbonite. It is interesting that although he is handcuffed going into the machine, when he comes out encased in Carbonite, his hands are free, and he is in the crucifixion pose of Jesus on the Cross. Years go by (we don't know how many but at least 3, representing the 3 days), and Solo is freed from his prison, or cave of carbonite, only to be reborn again or resurrected.

Images from "Star Wars: The Empire Strikes Back" (1980) and "Star Wars: The Return of the Jedi" (1984)

Yoda is also an interesting character from the Star Wars saga, introduced in the second installment, The Empire Strikes Back. Like many of Joseph Campbell's writings, especially "The Hero with 1000 Faces" (1949), we are introduced to the path of the Tarot, where a young fool (Luke) embarks on a journey. Along the way, he meets a mentor or two (Kenobi and then Yoda and eventually his own father Anakin), who shows him a little more of the path and the way of the force. Yoda is an interesting character because of what his name and look imply. His look is borrowed from the 14th Century "Smithfield Decretals of Gregory IX". This is an interesting book because amongst its passages are depicted animals in humanistic form or anthropomorphs, animals taking human form and thus telling a broader story of morals and values.

However, amongst the pages is a depiction of a Yoda-like creature, clad in an orange robe of the monks and sporting Yoda's ears and webbed digits for fingers. No one really knows what this creature is, but in this book, he is talked about as being all knowledgeable, a Yoda persona.

We also find that in the "Star Wars: The Mandalorian" (2019) adventures by Disney/Lucas Films, there is a young Yoda-like creature. As Yoda belongs to a classification of species in the Star Wars Universe as "species unknown," we can only speculate that this species shares a strong connection to the Force. Grogu, as the new character is named, is an interesting choice of names. Grogu is a masculine name of American origin, meaning "the child," which he is called throughout the storyline. Yoda, as a name, also comes from another name of similar expression, that of the Hebrew letter Yod. Yod is the 10th letter of the Hebrew alphabet. As we know from number symbology, 10 means completeness, finality, and perfection, but also has another significance in Hebrew as it means "a divine point of energy" and is also the symbol of the iconic "S" on Superman's chest. Also of interest, Superman's name is Kal-El, which not only has Saturnian symbolism to it but is also a derivative of El or the name of God. Kal-El, therefore, means the "Voice of God," and as Krypton was destroyed in the ancient story of Superman, it is interesting that Krypton was also the designation of the exploded planet in the Marduk, Tiamat story line of the ancient cosmic war and now makes up our asteroid belt.

Of other interesting planets of once and forgotten pasts and futures, we have the closest planet to the sun, closer than Mercury and discovered independently by 3 astronomers. Newton attributed Mercury's wobble to the gravitational influence of an additional planet. This hypothetical celestial body, named Vulcan, was initially sighted in 1859 and later affirmed by the prominent astronomer Urbain Le Verrier. The New York Times celebrated Vulcan as a significant discovery of the century. During the July 1878 eclipse, two prominent American astronomers, James Craig Watson and Lewis Swift, claimed to have seen Vulcan. However, today we are told that there is no planet Vulcan, and even in the reboot of Star Trek, they allude to this as a once and future planet by destroying it. As we seem to know so much but really so little about our own solar system, galaxy, and even universe, we are short to claim that this planet doesn't exist. Having one astronomer sight it is one thing but to have 3 independently is a whole another level of disclosure to its existence. Just to throw more water on the fire, Earth has a second moon that we never talk about ever. Confirmed in 2021 (though discussed for over 25 years), Earth's second moon is a quasi-satellite called Kamoʻoalewa (meaning: a part of a Hawaiian chant and alludes to an offspring that travels on its own). Despite its significance, this information is not widely known, possibly due to the complexity surrounding the facts about our planet's additional celestial companion.

Another Star Wars Saga of interest is the TV Show "Star Wars: Andor" (2022), where in the first season one of the "rebels" is injured and taken to surgery. He is operated on by an alien being, bald, with eye goggles, and ear coverings, as well as 4 arms that we can see, helping stitch back together the wounded. It is interesting that traveling to Peru, in 2014 I came across a few anomalous artifacts showing out-of-place items, ideas, and cultures. One such was a piece of pottery, a vase, or ceremonial clay gourd depicting almost the same scene. This is not coincidence, though I cannot prove that the Star Wars: Andor creators did not borrow from such an artifact, I do find it dubious as it is hidden in a back room on a shelf of hundreds of other artifacts to be signaled out unless the TV show creators of today had the same vigorous study of the occult that WW2 German Ahnenerbe did, doubtful but still interesting.

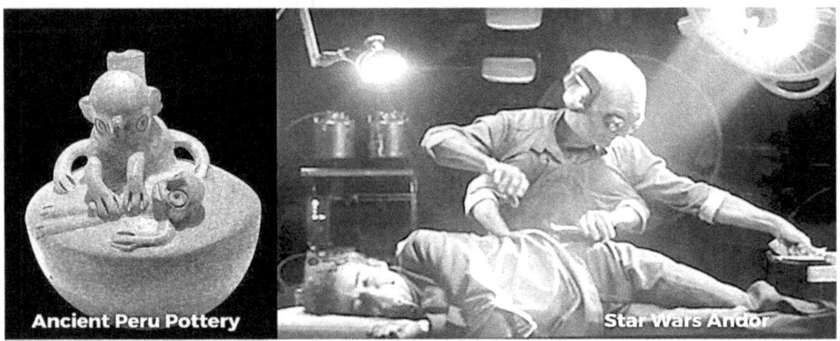

Of note: Heinrich Himmler established the Ahnenerbe in 1935 as a branch of the SS, tasked with researching ancient cultures and practices.

Among the artifacts found in the same collection in Peru, intriguing references emerge, including depictions related to the Kama Sutra, dragons (from Asia), and woolly mammoths (from regions much further north). In the Gold Museum, a tapestry of symbolism unfolds, connecting ancient Egypt/Khemit with the golden headdresses of Amun. These artifacts bear a curious relationship to "Incan Ceremonial Burial Headdresses," evidently influenced by Egyptian aesthetics.

Venturing deeper into this cultural crossroads, an Egyptian Admiral of the Seas named Maui or Ma'wi comes to light, documented in hieroglyphs from Egypt/Khemit associated with Ramses II at Karnak. Remarkably, Maui's maritime exploits date back to 300 BC or even earlier, unveiling a historical narrative that transcends time. His voyages connected Polynesia all the way to Alaska through Hawaii, a fascinating odyssey detailed in the enlightening documentary "Under the Carpet: Skeletons in the

Cupboards: Where did the Red Heads Go." This compelling series unravels the ancestral lineage of the Maori people in New Zealand, establishing connections to regions like Azerbaijan and Iran, tracing back thousands of years.

The headress of Amun as found in Egypt and Peru, Larco Gold Museum, Lima Peru.

Moving forward, another captivating theme prevalent in recent movies, particularly from 1984 onwards, is the symbolic use of whales. As humans, our understanding of these majestic creatures is limited. Personally, I contributed to tracking whales during my 5th and 6th-grade years. However, a more profound encounter unfolded when I resided on Maui from 2009 to 2011, and again in 2013, when I had the remarkable opportunity to swim within 100 feet of two humpback whales. The experience, though initially intimidating due to strong currents near volcanic rock cliffs, proved awe-inspiring, making the risk worthwhile.

The significance of whales in cinema is intriguing. In the 1986 film "Star Trek IV: The Voyage Home," the crew embarks on a time-travel mission to retrieve two humpback whales, crucial for saving the human race. The storyline unfolds as an ancient race of cetaceans returns to its Earth colony, seeking to understand the events that nearly led to humanity's destruction.

Contrastingly, in the expansive galaxy of "Star Wars," specifically in the "Rebels" (2014-2018) finale, a different kind of cetacean-like beings called the Purrgil takes center stage. These bio-engineered hybrids, combining elements of whales and squids, are designed to gracefully navigate the vastness of space. Their extraordinary ability to effortlessly enter hyperspace allows them to traverse light-years in an instant.

In related narratives, Ezra captures Thrawn in the Rebels finale, sending him to the unknown reaches of the galaxy's outer rims. In "Ahsoka" (2023), both Ahsoka and Sabine Wren journey to uncharted territories to rendezvous with Ezra and Thrawn. Notably, Thrawn's crew and stormtroopers are labeled the 332, a reference to the number 8 and Thrawn's family, the Eighth Ruling Family of the Chiss. The incorporation of gold face plates and parts aligns with the golden body symbolism in Buddhism, achieved through dream capabilities and acceptance.

Grand Admiral Thrawn depicted with his 332 army of zombie troopers commanded by captain Enoch with his gold helmet "Ahsoka" (2023).

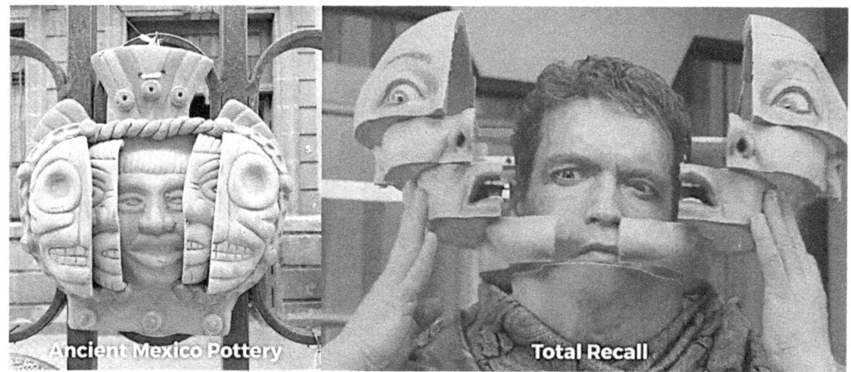

In the Science fiction movie "Total Recall" (1990), we have a depiction of the 3 faced nesting doll of "The Sun". A ceramic piece with three faces, adorned with 13 circular gems, or chalchihuitl, evoking the 13 months of the sacred calendar. Interestingly this is very similar to the splitting head motif found in "Total Recall" when the character of Quaid (portrayed by Arnold Schwarzenegger) removes his mask at the Mars airport. Of more interest, most of this movie was filmed in Mexico City which could have given rise to such imagery.

In the DC film "Black Adam" (2022), there is use of the triangle hand sign created by placing both hands together connecting at the thumbs and forefinger with palms facing out, emphasizing its origins in Freemasonry and its representation of the triangle of power. The broader exploration of esoteric knowledge in movies includes titles like Blade Runner famous for using "eyes", Inception and its "dream" symbology, Interstellar with its " Saturnian" symbology, "Hellraiser" with the "Pandora's Box" reference that we also find in the "Tomb Raider" movies and even the "Mother Boxes" found in the "DC: Justice League" (2017) movie.

The "Mother Boxes" from DC's "Justice League" (2017).

There are also what we know as symbolic predictive programmed events. Numerous theorists assert that fictional media undergoes manipulation through a phenomenon known as "predictive programming." This process is believed to involve incorporating references to planned false flags, upcoming technological advancements, social transformations, and other events anticipated in the future. These events become symbolic due to the ability to revisit timestamps of publication and observe how closely current events align with predictions.

Classic examples include the "Back to the Future" trilogy (1985, 1989, and 1990), which predicted events of October 2015. While these events did not occur as forecasted, the franchise did accurately predict certain aspects, such as franchising, social media, portable home technology, retro 80s nostalgia, targeted advertising, and hydrators. Notably, the conspiracy theory linking "Back to the Future," 9-11, and the movie "The Wire" (2015) adds an intriguing layer, connecting Marty McFly's attire to a tight wire walker in "The Wire."

Predictive programming and current day revealing of the method also find their way into both the James Bond and Mission Impossible franchises. In "Diamonds are Forever" (1971), James Bond tracks down an illegal diamond smuggling ring, discovering a film set in a Nevada Desert facility (reminiscent of Area 51) faking a moon landing mission and weaponizing space with diamond-based space lasers. This is seen as a nod to the conspiracy theory around the moon landing being a theatrical performance.

"Diamonds are Forever" (1971) James Bond on the moon set, in the Nevada desert at the height of the Apollo program.

The illegal diamond theme recurs in "Die Another Day" (2002), where the main villain Gustav Graves, possibly based on Elon Musk, plans to use conflict diamonds in a satellite laser-weapon system named Icarus. The media's subsequent treatment of Musk, demonizing his character and even equating him to the anti-Christ, is seen because of predictive programming.

In "Casino Royale" (2006), a reveal of the method occurs when "M" admits to put options placed on the two airlines involved in the 9-11 attacks, suggesting insider trading among those privy to the terror plot. "Quantum of Solace" (2008) reveals an interesting plot involving underground water reservoirs in South America, tied to real-world events like the Bush family's land acquisition in Paraguay over a significant water aquifer.

The water theme, predictive programmed in both the book and movie "Three Days of the Condor" (1975), predicting future conflicts over water resources, reappears in various TV series and movies, including "Star Trek Voyager" (1995) and "Avatar 2: The Way of Water" (2022).

Despite the symbolic predictive and reveal programming in most James Bond franchise movies, the Mission Impossible franchise also incorporates esoteric and occult ideas. In the recent "Mission: Impossible - Dead Reckoning Part One" (2023), the concept of the "cruciform cross key" emerges, referencing the Brotherhood of the Cruciform Sword seen first in "Indiana Jones and the Last Crusade" (1989). This key symbolizes unlocking the codes of AI, referred to as "the Entity" or fallen child, seeking to take over the world, to become the new God. The characters Gabriel, the announcer of God's presence, and Grace as in the Grace of God, both biblical references, add depth to the narrative, exploring AI's role in humanity, revealing a thought-provoking layer to the Mission Impossible storyline.

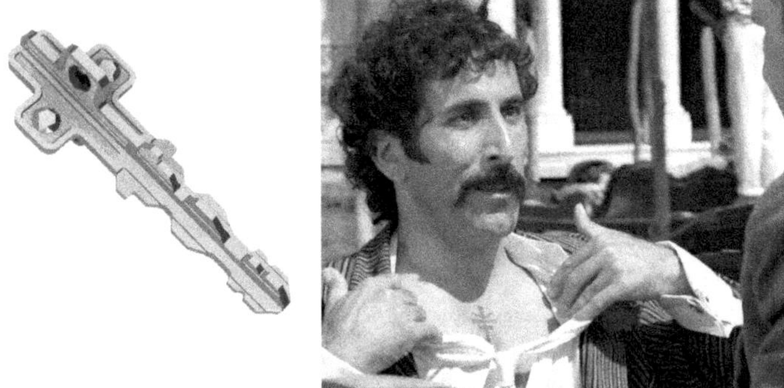

The Cruciform Cross Key from "Mission: Impossible - Dead Reckoning Part One" (2023), and the Brotherhood of the Cruciform Sword as seen in "Indiana Jones and the Last Crusade" (1989)

Mystery School Symbology

A further exploration of symbols and symbology leads us to the esoteric symbolism of the Free Masonic Order, and other mystery Schools such as the Rosicrucian Order and the Order of the Knights Templar. These symbols found in various logos is extensive and touches on a wide range of esoteric concepts. Here's a summary of some key observations:

Egyptian/Khemetian hieroglyph for Sirius.

1. **Sirius Symbolism in Freemasonry:**
    - Sirius is revered as the "blazing sun" in Freemasonry.
    - Ancient Egyptian depictions associate Sirius with an obelisk, a dome, and the blazing star.
    - By comparison, Masonic symbols include the blazing star of Sirius, obelisks, the pillars of Joachim and Boaz, and the temple dome.
    - The checkered board on the temple floor or the Masonic pavement symbolizes the duality of light and dark and represents the earth, while the ceiling represents the sky and heavens.

Infamous Skull and Bones, Jolly Roger with 322 numerology related to mastering alignment with a greater power, knowing good and evil.

2. **Masonic Pirates of the Caribbean:**

    - The Jolly Roger, Skull and Bones, and the symbol of Pirates are associated with Masonic special forces, the Pirates of the Caribbean.
    - These pirates targeted English and Spanish Armada galleons to secure treasures for the Masonic cause.

Official Worldwide Emblem of the Rosicrucian Order.

3. **The Rosicrucian Order:**

The Rosicrucian tradition encompasses a complex and esoteric system of symbolism that has evolved over centuries. Rooted in the teachings of the mysterious Rosicrucian Brotherhood, this symbology combines elements of mysticism, alchemy, astrology, and spiritual philosophy. A synopsis of Rosicrucian symbology might highlight key themes:

- **The Rose and the Cross:**

  The central symbols of the Rosicrucian tradition are the rose and the cross. The rose represents spiritual unfoldment, enlightenment, and the unfolding of the inner self. The cross, often a Christian cross, symbolizes sacrifice, resurrection, and the integration of spiritual and material aspects of existence.

- **The Alchemical Process:**

  Rosicrucian symbology often incorporates alchemical motifs, reflecting the transformative journey of the soul. The stages of alchemy—nigredo (blackening), albedo (whitening), citrinitas (yellowing), and rubedo (reddening)—are seen as metaphors for personal and spiritual growth.

- **The Labyrinth:**

  Symbolizing the winding path of self-discovery and enlightenment, the labyrinth is a common motif. It represents the journey of the soul through the twists and turns of life, leading to a deeper understanding of one's purpose and connection to the divine.

- **Astrological Symbols:**

  Astrological symbolism is integral to Rosicrucian

teachings, linking cosmic forces to individual spiritual development. Planetary symbols and the zodiac are often employed to convey the interconnectedness of the microcosm (individual) and macrocosm (universe).

- **Hermetic Principles:**

  The seven Hermetic Principles, such as "As above, so below," are fundamental to Rosicrucian thought. These principles reflect the idea of universal interconnectedness and the correspondence between different planes of existence.

- **The Philosopher's Stone:**

  As a quintessential alchemical symbol, the Philosopher's Stone represents the culmination of spiritual and mystical transformation. It embodies the transmutation of base elements into spiritual gold, symbolizing the attainment of higher consciousness.

- **Sacred Geometry:**

  Geometric symbols, such as the vesica piscis, the Flower of Life, and the golden ratio, are used to convey fundamental truths about the structure of the cosmos and the inherent order in creation.

- **The Emerald Tablet:**

  The Emerald Tablet, attributed to Hermes Trismegistus, is a key text in Hermeticism and Rosicrucianism. Its famous saying, "As above, so below; as below, so above," encapsulates the interconnectedness of the spiritual and material realms.

In summary, Rosicrucian symbology weaves together a rich tapestry of mystical and philosophical elements, aiming to guide practitioners on a transformative journey toward spiritual enlightenment and understanding of the deeper mysteries of existence.

The Grand Masters of the Knights Templar during the later 12th and the 13th century used a double-sided seal which showed a representation of The Dome of the Rock (or a circular dome of the Church of the Holy Sepulcher) on one side, and the Order's symbol of two knights on one horse on the other side.

4. **Order of the Knights Templar:** (**co-written with Timothy Hogan, Grand Master of the Templar Order, OTSI Lineage**)

   - **Foundation of the Templar Order** (**Around 1100 CE**):

     Purpose: The Templar Order was founded with the primary goal of seeking remnants of ancient philosophy, technology, and knowledge, particularly associated with a pre-diluvian civilization linked to Noah and Atlantis.

   - **Associations with Gnostic Lineages** (**Middle East and Europe**):

     The Templars established associations with Gnostic lineages across the Middle East and Europe, indicating a broad network for their pursuits.

- **Archaeological Endeavors in Jerusalem, Lebanon, and Egypt:**

  The Templars engaged in extensive archaeological activities in Jerusalem, Lebanon, and Egypt, likely in search of ancient knowledge and artifacts.

- **Suppression by the Roman Church and French Monarchy (1307):**

  In 1307, the Templars faced suppression by the Roman Church and the French Monarchy, leading them to go underground.

- **Formation of the Rosicrucian Movement and Influence on Freemasonry:**

  After their suppression, the Templars played a role in the formation of the Rosicrucian movement and influenced the development of Freemasonry.

- **Creation of Other Orders, Including Militia Cruceferia Evangelica:**

  The Templars also gave rise to other orders, such as the Militia Cruceferia Evangelica in Wittenberg, Germany.

- **Name Change to Knights of Christ in Germany:**

  In Germany, the Templars adopted the name "Knights of Christ."

- **Transmission of Knowledge to Europe:**

  The Templars brought back alchemical, Qabbalistic, Hermetic, and Gnostic doctrines to Europe, which they inscribed on Gothic cathedrals, contributing to their construction.

- **Symbol of the Red Equal-Armed Cross:**

  The Templars' symbol, the red equal-armed cross, had ancient origins, appearing in Sumerian and Egyptian contexts, and passed down through Coptic and Albigensian traditions. The cross symbolized the spiritual and physical worlds, representing the idea of "spiritualizing the material and materializing the spiritual through the medium of consciousness."

- **Connections with Indigenous Cultures in the Americas:**

  The Templars established connections with indigenous cultures in the Americas before Columbus's arrival, indicating a broader scope of their activities and influence.

The doorknob of a Templar temple in Germany from the late 1500s.

In summary, the Templar Order's history involves a multifaceted journey that encompasses archaeological pursuits, suppression, underground activities, the formation of influential movements, and connections with diverse spiritual and cultural traditions.

Tibetan tryptic symbol for the Cintamani stone.

5. **Theosophists and Cintamani Stone:**

   - Theosophists, including Helena Petrovna Blavatsky, Alice Bailey, Nicholas Roerich sought esoteric knowledge in regions like Afghanistan, Pakistan, Kashmir, Ladakh, India, Nepal, and Tibet.
   - The Cintamani stone, believed to be a piece of meteor from Sirius, was sought as a symbolic link to Mt. Meru and Sirius through the pineal and crown chakras.
   - Theosophy's ideas connect the inner earth city of Shambhala, where the Cintamani stone is said to reside, to Afghanistan and Tibet.

Helena Petrovna Blavatsky, Alice Bailey, & Nicholas Roerich.

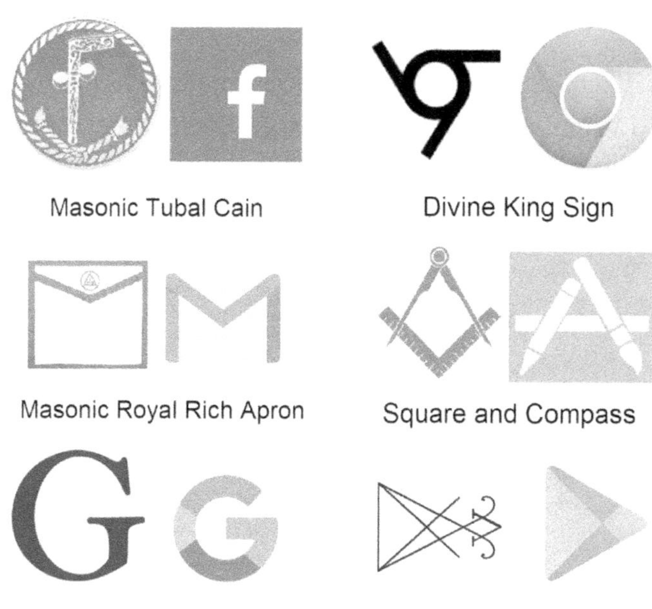

6. **Masonic-Based Logos:**

   - Facebook's logo represents Masonic Tubal Cain and the symbolism of 007, which was also the symbol of Queen Elizabeth's court alchemist, spy and magician, John Dee, which gave rise to the 007 symbology behind James Bond and the Mason behind his handler "M".

   - Google Chrome's logo is associated with the "Divine King" and the concept of 666.

   - The Gmail logo features elements of the Masonic Royal Rich Apron.

   - The App Store logos exhibit Masonic Compass and Square symbology.

   - The "G" in Google is associated with Masonic phrases like "God Geometrizes Greatness" and Plato's "God

Geometrizes Continually."

- The Google Play logo has a resemblance to the "Seal of Lucifer" or the Seal of Satan, with a distinction between Lucifer and Satan explained.
- The checkered floor of the BMW logo and the Knights Templar cross and serpent of the Alpha Romeo logo also come to mind, as seen below.

The BMW checkered floor and Alpha Romeo Knight's Templar red and white cross and the Crowned Serpent.

This investigation into Mystery School symbology takes us on a fascinating journey that probes the interconnections among esoteric symbols, ancient mysteries, and contemporary corporate logos. The core of this exploration is to unveil the concealed meanings and intricate relationships that exist within these diverse realms, providing a distinctive viewpoint to unravel the significance of these symbols.

Mystery School symbology, deeply rooted in history, represents a rich tapestry of esoteric knowledge and profound insights. These symbols, shrouded in mystery and deliberately obscured for the uninitiated, encapsulate the wisdom of ancient traditions and spiritual depths. By delving into this symbolic language, one embarks on a quest to decode the enigmatic messages passed down through generations, transcending time and cultural boundaries. The convergence with modern corporate logos introduces a captivating dimension, where inspiration from ancient symbols shapes contemporary visual identities, prompting reflection on the enduring influence of ancient wisdom in our present-day world.

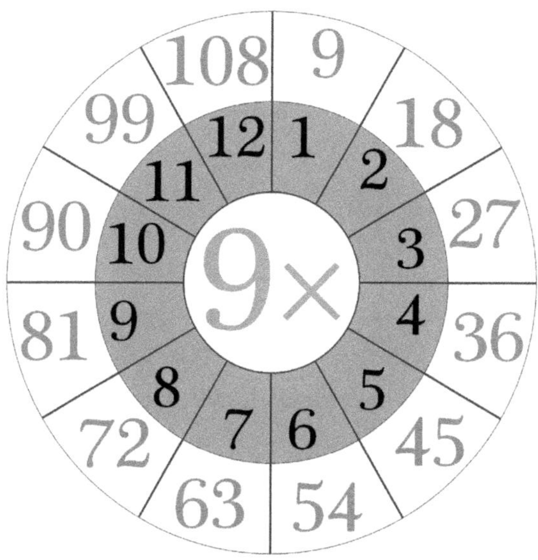

The Magic of the Number 9

The exploration of the number 9 in various cultural, philosophical, and symbolic contexts is indeed fascinating. Here's a summary of the rich associations with the number 9:

1. **Spiritual Enlightenment and Completion:**
    - The number 9 is considered a symbol of spiritual enlightenment and completion, contrasting with the ongoing and infinite nature of the number 8.
2. **Master Number:**
    - 9 is a master number, and all components equal 9, demonstrating its unique properties in simple maths.

3. **Humanity and Birth:**
    - The number 9 represents humanity, as humans spend approximately 9 months in the womb before birth.
4. **Jehovah's Witnesses:**
    - In Jehovah's Witnesses beliefs, only 144,000 souls can be saved and go to heaven, and the number 144 reduces to 9 (1 + 4 + 4).
5. **Chinese Philosophy:**
    - In Chinese philosophy, the number 9 is associated with magical dragons, and there are 9 types of dragons. Dragons in Chinese culture have 117 scales, with 81 being yin (heavenly) and 36 being yang (earthly). The number 9 is linked to Chinese legends, magic, and even medicine.
6. **Chinese Medicine:**
    - In Chinese medicine, there are 9 points and channels to the heart, symbolizing the art of healing and immortality.
7. **Hong Kong and 9gag:**
    - Kowloon in Hong Kong means the nine dragons, symbolizing the dragon as a representation of the Chinese emperor. The social media company 9gag, based in Hong Kong, incorporates a stylized 9 in its logo, playing with positive and negative space to create a cube/broken hexagon, which carries Saturnian symbology.
8. **Yin and Yang:**
    - The spinning positive-negative 9 in yin-yang symbology represents duality and opposites, offering a profound perspective on balance and harmony.

The multifaceted associations of the number 9 across different cultures and belief systems showcase its symbolic richness and the diverse ways it is integrated into various aspects of human understanding and expression.

The 9GAG media logo from Hong Kong representing a stylized 9, a G hidden in the 9 shape and a cube hidden beneath both.

Similarly in Hindu belief there are 9 influences on traditional Vedic astrology, as well as 9 universal elements made up of; earth, water, air, fire, either, time, space, soul and mind, elements borrowed heavily with the 6 infinity stones that come out of Marvel comics Infinity War saga. There are 9 forms of the goddess Durga, master of protection, strength, motherhood, destruction, and wars, and she is thus celebrated over the course of 9 days. Also of note are the 9 jewels or Navaratnas were political figures that often surrounded the Indian King's as their advisors.

The significance of the number 9 and its multiples, such as 108, in various cultures is indeed fascinating. The practice of folding 108 origami cranes for good luck in Japanese culture and its connection to the number 9, as pointed out, reflects a symbolic and auspicious meaning.

In Tibetan culture, the association of 108 with the volumes of the words of the Buddha and the use of malas (prayer beads) with 108 beads further emphasizes the cultural and spiritual importance of this number. The repetition of mantras using a mala is a common practice in Tibetan Buddhism, and the use of 108 beads in this context aligns with the broader cultural significance of the number.

These cultural practices highlight how numbers, including their multiples and combinations, can take on symbolic meanings that transcend mere mathematical significance. They become woven into the fabric of cultural traditions and spiritual practices, carrying with them layers of meaning and significance that contribute to the richness of these traditions. It can be found in Egyptian cultures, Greek mythology, even Mayan tales of the underworld which most closely relate to Dante's 9 circles of hell also known as the 9 gates; limbo (a space reserved for the unbaptized and virtuous pagans), then lust, gluttony, greed, anger, heresy, violence, and lastly fraud.

9 is a number found in time magic and meaning. 09:09 is a mirror hour, representing the expression "the best is yet to come" and plays on the understanding of intuition, or listening to your "small" or "inner voice", often representing complexity, inner life, humanism, and searching, and can also represent loneliness invading your daily life or spiritually your guardian angel is trying to surround you with good people.

9 also has biblical and horoscopic meaning. 9 is the month of September, the beginning of the harvest and is symbolized by the Virgo, or virgin, a young maiden carrying a sheaf of wheat. In the bible (chapters 36-39) the 9th month is a season for winning battles through prayer, a month of changes and is represented by a rainbow of peace in genesis 9, however not being a biblical scholar, I cannot go into much depth about this.

Even Nicolai Tesla had a fascination with 9 as his attempts to connect to a higher power came through the numbers 3, 6 and 9 which if added up make 18, where 8 + 1 is 9. According to Tesla, the numbers 3, 6, and 9 are unique in their ability to exist as energy without losing their fundamental identity. This idea finds support in modern physics, where these numbers play a significant role in the examination of atomic and subatomic particles. The number 9 stands out among most numbers due to its profound and historical connections to astrology, magic, science, and philosophy.

33 As a Magical Number

The magic of the number 33 is also significant as this is the number of the master mason. A 33° Mason is a Master Mason who has exhibited knowledge, passion, and sacrifice to the craft. There are 33 vertebrae in the spine with the head or crown being the 33, which also represents the steps a mason will go through to become a master mason.

Walt Disney, who may or may not have been a Mason, created in 1967, Club 33 which resides above the pirates of the Caribbean ride at the park. This is significant because pirates were also considered master masons and flew the skull and bones flag to show their allegiance to the craft, especially the Skull and bones society, from which several prominent people in US history including the late George HW Bush, and his father Prescott Bush, his son George W Bush and even John Kerry, who all have had some controversial histories to say the least. It is interesting that Though I have heard that Disneyland sits on the 33rd degree north parallel of the planet, it does not, but instead San Diego to the south does, as does Dallas Texas where President Kennedy was assassinated. Of interest, Kennedy was killed on 11/22 on the 33rd degree, which seems of ritualistic symbology. It is interesting that Tripoli Libya, Damascus Syria and even Baghdad Iraq, all places of geopolitical interest in recent years, sit on this parallel line.

It is further regarded as a magical number bridging the realms of the everyday and the spiritual, associated with attributes such as compassion, inspiration, discipline, and honesty. In the Vedic tradition of India, there are 33 deities in their pantheon of gods and goddesses. Like numbers 8, 9, 10, and 11, the number 33 is recognized as a master number, signifying guidance, and symbolizing the belief that all things are achievable.

SpaceX pictures of the heavy lift launch vehicle and its 33 rockets.

It's noteworthy that SpaceX highlights the use of 33 Raptor engines in their recent, albeit unsuccessful, attempt to launch Starship into space—a subtle nod to those familiar with esoteric symbolism. While Elon Musk's affiliation with Freemasonry remains unknown, as Masons typically operate discreetly, the conspicuous use of the number 33 suggests a potential connection to Masonic themes in space exploration. It is interesting that if we look at the name Elon as a symbolic representation, we can break it into two words, "El" meaning God and "On" meaning star or sun. Thus, Elon means the God Star or God Sun (son).

United Nations emblem and flag displaying the 33 segments.

The number 33 holds significance in the United Nations global flag and emblem, marked by the presence of 33 segments within the inner circle. Despite its intended symbolism, this emblem has been misinterpreted by some, notably the Flat Earth Society, as a representation of the world map. In reality, the 33 segments symbolize the eight cardinal points extending from the central ring, signifying the founding members of the United Nations and their connection to other nations and continents in what was originally named the League of Nations.

Richard Hoagland and Mike Bara delve into the secrets of NASA's history in their influential book, "Dark Mission: The Secret History of NASA." The revelations shed light on the founding members of NASA, introducing figures like Jack Parsons, associated with JPL and a follower of Aleister Crowley, and Theodore Von Karmen. Notably, the organization included individuals with connections to the SS, such as Werner von Braun, Humbertus Strughold, and Kurt Debus. These figures, despite their association with war crimes, had their records expunged through "Project Paperclip," adding a controversial layer to the history of NASA.

In essence, the number 33 becomes a symbol not only in the visual representation of the United Nations but also in the complex historical web woven around the founding of NASA and its key figures.

278 *Dark Mission*

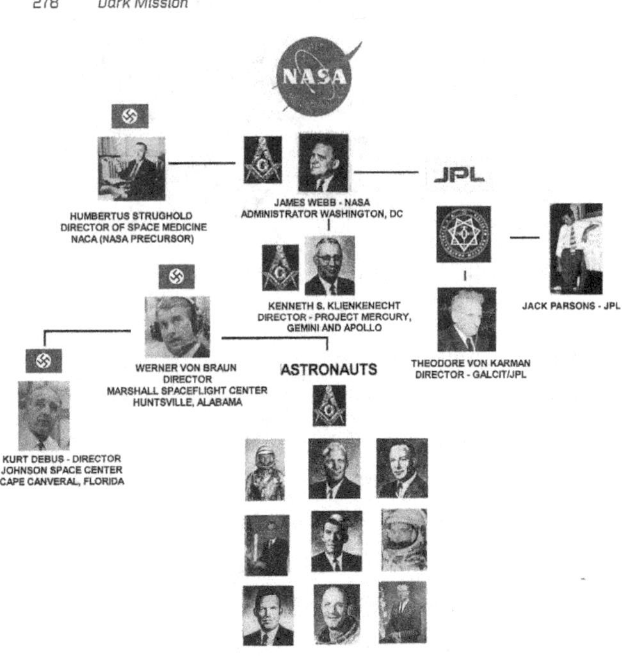

Fig. 5-28 - Organization chart showing Masons, SS members and "magicians" in key positions of power all throughout NASA in the 1960s. Everybody who was anybody at the Agency, from the director on down, was a member of one of these three secret cults.

Page 278 from Dark Mission: The Secret History of NASA (2007), Fig. 5-28 showing the Nazis, Masons and Magicians who established NASA in its early conception.

Considering the Masonic influence throughout NASA's history, from leaders like James Webb and Kenneth S. Kleinknecht to many astronauts, the choice of 33 rocket engines by SpaceX prompts speculation about the intended audience for this symbolic display.

In Werner von Braun's 1953 book "Mars Project: A Technical Tale," a prophecy emerges about the colonization of Mars, led by an individual named Elon. Notably, Elon Musk's SpaceX reusable rocket program appears to draw parallels with OTRAG, a secretive German rocket initiative exposed by President Gorbachev in 1976, operating in the Congo (Zaire).

OTRAG is yet another Saturnian logo/symbol and is depicted in the company's orange color.

OTRAG and the SpaceX Starship comparison, both utilizing "reusable" rockets, which to date are not reusable as initially promoted.

The James Webb Space Telescope stands out as the latest addition to our space exploration toolkit, offering an enhanced ability to gaze further into the universe with unprecedented clarity. The profound advancements in vision it provides invite endless speculation and discussion. On the surface, the various elements seem to interconnect, weaving a captivating narrative that sparks curiosity and raises intriguing questions about the mysteries of the cosmos.

WEBB

It is intriguing to note that in the original logo of the James Webb Space Telescope, there is a blend of Saturnian symbolism through the inclusion of 19 hexagons (9 + 1 = 10 representing the completed work or perfection in magical numerology) and a depiction of the satellite observing the radiant star Sirius. Once more, these symbols seem to be subtly hidden in plain sight, adding an element of mystique to the mission.

666 Symbology

Another interesting number that constantly comes up in symbology is 666, often thought to Christianity as the mark of the beast or the number of a man. It has a much older and esoteric value in magical numbers, referring to luck in Chinese culture, and combined makes 18 which is also the number 9, the number of months we spend in the womb. To those in the know the actual mark of the beast is a X with a circle around it which can be found in the X-men logo, and ironically also in the Xbox logo, and interestingly one of the ancient symbols for KMT or Khemit.

666 however can be found in several corporate logos either through visual numerology (unlike gematria), shapes and symbols, or even occult or hidden. A few logos that come to mind are the Century Link logo, we discussed earlier, which has 6 light green triangles and 6 dark green triangles and then the space between is an asterisk of negative space with 6 lines. However, in simple gematria "CenturyLink" = 152, where 1 + 5 + 2 = 8, and we are back to the infinity representation in the wordmark and thus business practice of fiber connectivity being infinitely available.

The second logo that comes to mind is the FOX logo. If we take the letters F, O, and X we discover that F is the 6th letter of the alphabet, O is the 15th letter where 1 + 5 = 6, and X is the 24th letter where 2 + 4 = 6 all spelling out a 666 connection. On a numeric keypad the numbers are 3, 6 and 9, Tesla's magical number set and 3 + 6 + 9 = 18 which then = 9, much like 6 + 6 + 6 = 18 and 1 + 8 = 9, so we keep coming back to these interesting magical number strings. Additionally, the Fox has its own symbology, and are often represent cunning, playfulness, and resilience. Foxes walk the fine line between the wilderness and urban living, making the best of both environments. They are adaptable, clever, and full of mischief, tricksters.

The FOX logo bathed in a pyramid of search lights subtly symbolizes the pyramid and all seeing eye.

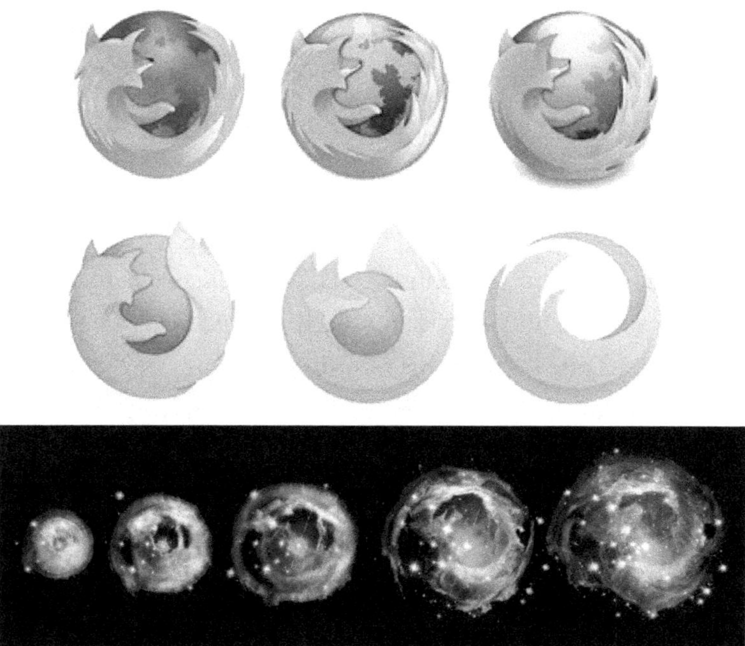

V838 Monocerotis stages of expansion beginning from May 2002 to October 2004.

The Firefox logo bears a striking resemblance to the cosmic nebula V838 Monocerotis, which has been expanding since 2002 and intriguingly appears to be moving in the direction of Earth. While this resemblance could be a case of pareidolia—an inclination to perceive meaningful patterns where none exist—it is fascinating to note the visual similarity. The resemblance was significant enough that Mozilla, prompted by user concerns and the potential for backlash, decided to modify their logo over time, moving away from the fox-like imagery and the visual likeness to the V838 nebula. This evolution in the logo design reflects an interesting interplay between cosmic aesthetics and user perception.

The number 666 can be subtly perceived in the Google Chrome logo, forming a vortex of three hidden 6s. This intriguing observation adds a layer of symbolism to the logo's design, inviting speculation about intentional or coincidental elements incorporated into the visual representation.

The Google Chrome 666 representation.

We also can look at the controversial Walt Disney signature proudly hiding the 666 symbology within it. Although a stretch of the imagination, we find this 666 used to promote "The Art of Disney" stores at the Disney theme parks, where ironically their slogan is "Capturing the Imagination."

The hidden 666 found in the Walt Disney signature is interestingly displayed as 666 in association with "The Art of Disney" shop at the Disney theme parks.

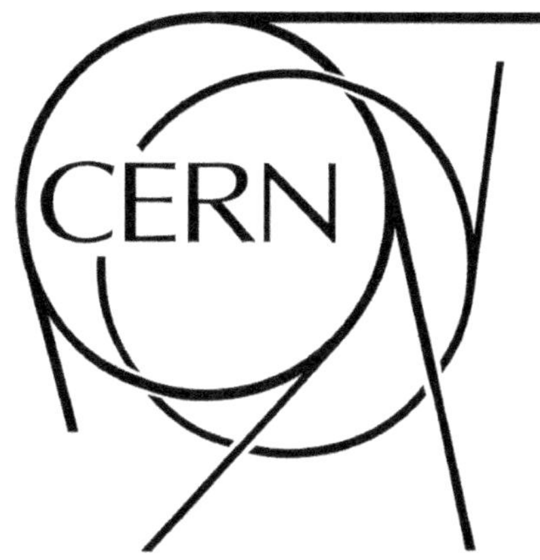

CERN logo showing the overlapping 666 symbology.

It is of interest that the CERN logo and emblem established in 1954, displays the inverted overlapping 666 symbology, which represents the Alice, Atlas, and Large Hadron Collider (LHCB). Alice is in reference to "Alice in Wonderland, a Walt Disney animation from 1951, and book published by Lewis Carrol in 1865, and follow up book "Through the Looking Glass" which is in reference to time travel technology. Atlas is in reference to a Titan condemned to hold up the heavens or sky for eternity after the Titanomachy. And the LHC is in reference to atomic smashing to find the Higgs Boson "God" particle. Sitting in front of CERN is the ominous statue of Shiva, the Destroyer of Worlds and the Universe at the end of time.

While in August of 2016, a video went viral of a mock human sacrifice performed in the courtyard of CERN by its employees, in similar fashion to the "Cremation of Care" which is a mock child sacrifice performed at the Bohemian Grove in California by wealthy elites and world leaders. In both cases, the powers-that-be quickly called these a hoax even though there is enough evidence to show that both events have happened, one in ritual to Molech or Bael (Saturn the Reaper) and the other to Shiva the Destroyer. Overall CERN seems to have an interest in "time", giving us all great pause and concern.

Beyond the realm of number magic and symbolism, the historical and ongoing fascination with celestial bodies reveals an array of occult or hidden symbology. In ancient times, our ancestors gazed at the night sky with awe, constructing deities from interconnected star patterns that eventually evolved into the foundations of our horoscopes. Planets, too, were revered as gods and goddesses across various cultures, sharing similar interpretations and meanings that have persisted through the ages. This rich tapestry of celestial symbolism reflects the enduring human quest to find meaning and connection in the vast expanse of the cosmos.

Suns, Stars, and Sirius "Blazing Star" Symbology

In ancient Egypt, or Khemit as some prefer to call it, considering the Greek derivation of Egypt from the phrase "Het Ka Ptah", meaning the place where Ptah, the creator god and patron of Memphis, manifested in physical form (Ka), we encounter a rich tapestry of symbology. This symbolism encompasses the phases of the sun, the star Sirius, and various planets, including Mars and Saturn.

Mars holds particular interest, as reflected in the Arabic word for

Cairo, Al Qahirah, meaning Mars. Similarly, the city of Heliopolis, a Greek name replacing the ancient Souf or Khemetian, On, meaning "the sun," illustrates the interplay of linguistic transformations over time.

Delving into word casting or word magic, the name Solomon can be deconstructed into components from three different languages. In Latin, "Sol" means the sun; in Sanskrit, "Ohm" represents the first sound of God; and in Khemetian, "On" signifies the sun. This dissection suggests that Solomon's name could mean "the first sound of the sun gods," a concept resonant with his reputed ability to invoke, trap, and release demons.

Moreover, the name Solomon may be interpreted as "Sol Omon," implying an Oman or emanation of the sun. In an English offshoot, it could also be seen as "Solo Man," denoting singularity. The English language itself, with its capacity for creating spell-like words, is considered by some as a tool for casting spells on a broader population—a concept that we will revisit later in this discourse on word spells.

The symbolism of the sun in ancient Khem is fascinating, extending beyond the commonly known Ra to encompass five distinct phases. Contrary to the prevailing notion that "Ra" was the sole name for the sun in ancient Egypt, it represents only one phase in the intricate tapestry of solar symbolism.

The first phase is "Khepher," symbolized by the dung beetle or scarab pushing a ball of dung onto the horizon at dawn. This act mirrors the scarab's life cycle, where the eggs laid in the dung serve as a source of nourishment for the emerging scarabs, akin to the life-giving qualities of the morning sun. This phase is also encapsulated in the concept of "Horus on the horizon," signifying the birth of Horus—the term from which the English word "hours" is derived.

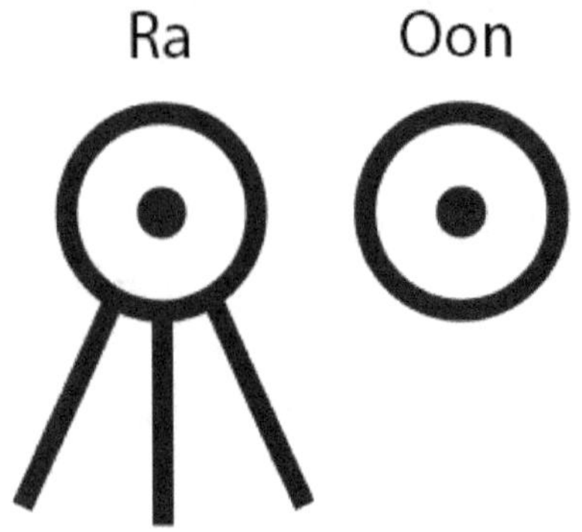

The second phase, known as "Ra," embodies the adolescent and rebellious energy of the morning sun. Following this, we encounter "Oon," representing the early afternoon sun, the wise, possibly influencing the English words "noon" and "afternoon".

The late afternoon sun is denoted by "Aten," symbolizing a state of enlightenment, the wiser, a golden age in both life and time. This phase inspired the name change of Amenhotep IV to Akhenaten, emphasizing his devotion to the sun god Aten, ushering in a new era of worship.

The final stage, "Amun," represents the hidden or darkness. Interestingly, the Christian prayer often concludes with the word "Amen," traditionally sealing the prayer in the hidden realms or darkness. This nuanced understanding adds depth to the symbolism associated with the sun in ancient Khem and sheds light on the layers of meaning embedded in seemingly commonplace practices.

In the Star Wars saga, specifically episodes IV, V, and VI, the character Luke Skywalker undergoes a hero's journey to save his father from the dark side of the Force, drawing parallels with Khemetian phases of the sun and Egyptian philosophy.

The name "Luke" is a derivative of "Lucius," meaning "the sun," and coupled with his last name "Skywalker," it signifies the sun walking across the sky. As Luke progresses through his journey and reaches the stage of Aten, equivalent to becoming a Jedi, the term "Jedi" itself finds its roots in the Khemetian word "Djed" or Djed pillar, symbolizing the spine of Osiris. The lightsaber's hilt, resembling the Djed pillar, further emphasizes the mastery of function associated with being a Jedi—a master of the functioning Force.

Upon reaching the Aten stage, Luke confronts his father on the horizon of darkness, symbolizing the battle between light and darkness. This echoes the ancient struggle between Horus and Seth, mirroring the conflict between the Jedi and the Sith in the Star Wars narrative. The confrontation culminates in Luke defeating his father, Darth Vader, through the darkness, ultimately vanquishing him with the light of a new day. In this transformation, Luke becomes the salvation or true son of his father, and Anakin, meaning warrior, evolves into a sun or light/astral being.

The Star Wars saga embeds esoteric knowledge and occult symbolism that may be easily overlooked in the entertainment value of the movies. To those initiated in such wisdom, the transfer of certain knowledge is evident, woven into the narrative for those attuned to recognize it.

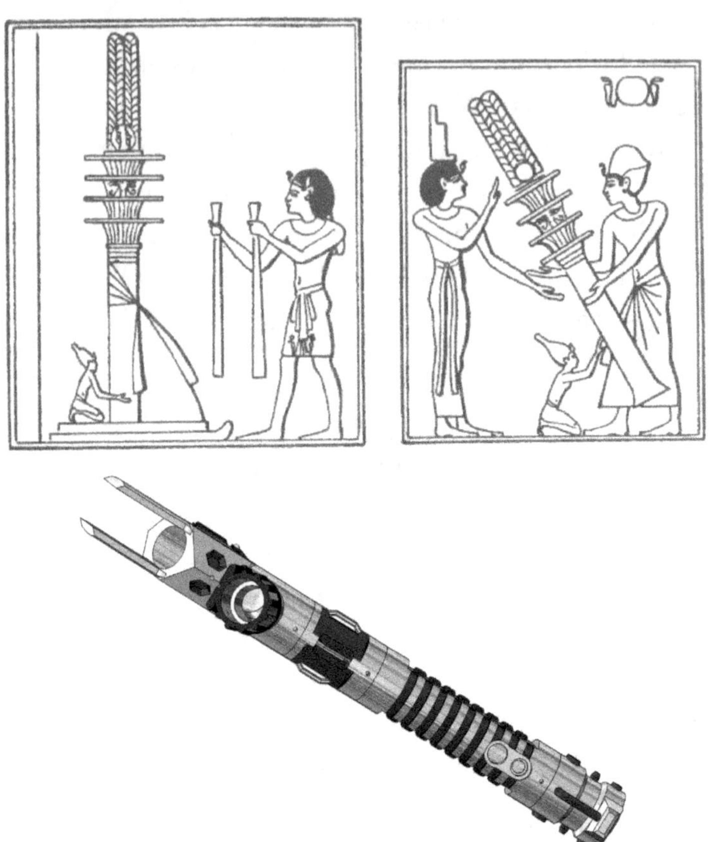

The Djed pillar of power and a lightsaber from the Star Wars saga. Both representing a similar power of duality and light energy.

Returning to Akhenaten and the symbolism of the sun, he is often depicted with a sun disk behind him, and the sun's rays extending with hands capped at their ends. This depiction underscores his association with solar symbology. Akhenaten's significance has transcended historical debates, with the Rosicrucian's venerating him as one of the divine forces behind all things. Throughout history, scholars have even contemplated whether Akhenaten could be identified as Moses, linked to the alleged theft of the Ark of the Covenant from the Great Pyramid—a symbolic event signifying a collapse of power across Egypt.

The sun, with its numerous rays, not only represents Akhenaten's reign but also holds significance in the symbolism of the blazing sun within Free Masonic orders. Interestingly, this blazing sun is connected to the star(s) of Sirius, a celestial body that discreetly appears in various corporate logos in modern times, cleverly hidden in plain sight. The subtle references to Sirius also extend into the realm of movies, suggesting a continuous thread of esoteric knowledge and symbolism woven into various aspects of human culture.

Twin Suns of Tatooine & Ahch-To from the Star Wars saga.

The symbolic reference to Sirius is intriguingly present in the Star Wars saga, with planets like Tatooine and Ahch-To featuring binary star systems reminiscent of Sirius. Additionally, in "The Truman Show," there's a noteworthy scene where a spotlight falls from the sky near Jim Carrey's character, Truman. As Truman lifts the spotlight, it reveals the word "Sirius" and "9 Canis Major" next to it.

Given that Sirius is part of the Canis Major constellation, often associated with the dog constellation, this raises an interesting question about the potential influence of Dog Star references on the modern naming of constellations, or vice versa. The interplay between cultural references, symbolism, and astronomical naming conventions adds depth to our understanding of how celestial objects have been woven into the fabric of human storytelling and imagination.

Depiction from The Truman Show discovering Sirius and Canis Major.

The symbolic reference to Sirius is widespread in various logos, subtly woven into the corporate and cultural fabric. For instance, Lockheed Martin and Sirius FM both incorporate Sirius in their logos, with the latter featuring a dog with a star for an eye, aligning with the historical association of Sirius as the Dog Star. Keanu Reeves' band, Dogstar, playfully nods to this masonic representation.

Incorporating sun and Sirius symbology, logos like OnStar evoke the name of Heliopolis or On, with Sirius being essentially a "sun star." Star TV, the lone star state of Texas, Texaco's star logo, Shell Gas with its seashell reminiscent of a blazing and rising sun, and BP's green and yellow sun logo all contribute to this thematic pattern. The US Army's logo, featuring a blazing star, and Converse shoes' logo of a star and chevron representing the blazing star moving through time further exemplify this trend.

Even the logo for the TV show and movie Stargate incorporates Sirius symbolism, with the singular sun dot over the "A" representing Sirius rising above the pyramids. These examples illustrate the prevalence of star and Sirius-related imagery in various logos, offering a glimpse into the rich tapestry of symbolism interwoven into modern culture and corporate branding.

Saturn Symbology

Saturn holds one of the most fascinating positions in occult planet or star symbology, deeply rooted in ancient religious practices and symbols, second only to the goddess worship of ancient times. In Greek mythology, Saturn was known as Chronos, the god of all gods. Chronos is often depicted with the scythe of the harvest, symbolizing the cyclical nature of time and the inevitable passage of all things. A darker aspect of the Chronos myth involves the unsettling image of him devouring his own children, a potent symbol of the relentless march of time and the inevitable destruction that it brings. This complex symbolism has resonated across various cultures and belief systems, contributing to Saturn's enduring significance in the occult.

Saturn, known as Bael, is associated with various symbols like the bull Moloch and the Baphomet, prevalent in pagan and satanic practices. The term "El," another name for Saturn, derives from Bael, and the city of Babylon, or Bae-el-bylon, is also connected to this deity, the city of Saturn.

In Roman culture, Saturn was highly revered, and Saturnalia, a festival held in the wintertime when Saturn was brightest in the sky, was celebrated in the city and lands of Saturnina (Rome). During Saturnalia, even slaves were allowed to partake in festivities, enjoying lavish meals, spirits, and table service. Saturn's day, Saturday, was dedicated to prayer.

In Indian mythology, Saturn is known as Shani, often depicted as a black god riding a crow, symbolizing rebirth. Shani is worshiped on Shani Vara, corresponding to Saturday. The multifaceted significance of Saturn is evident in its diverse representations across cultures and time periods.

Saturn depicted with the scythe of the harvest and injured and false left leg.

Bael, Moloch and the depiction of the Baphomet with children are all symbolic of Saturn the horned God of the sky.

Shani Bagwan depicted as a black God of resurrection the harvest and karma riding the crow as his chariot with injured left leg, similar to the depictions of Saturn.

Solomon's seal, a sigil that both entrances and ensnares demonic entities, later usurped by the Rothschild family as their symbol for the red shield, which then became the Zionist flag for Israel (Isis, Ra and El symbology of that name is interesting as well as it is symbolic of Lucifer the Sun God)

Saturn is associated with various symbols, including Solomon's seal, a sigil traditionally believed to capture and entrap demons. It is represented by two interlocking triangles, forming what is known today as the Star of David. This symbol, also adopted by the Rothschilds and associated with Zionism, has a hexagram at its center. The hexagon, a two-dimensional representation of a cube, is a geometric shape found at the core of the hexagram.

Interestingly, both cubes and hexagons have six sides, echoing the fact that Saturn is the sixth planet from the sun. At Saturn's poles, particularly its north pole, a remarkable and continuous dual and counter-rotating hexagonal storm system exists. Similar storm systems or anomalies are found on the north poles of other planets, but Saturn's hexagonal storm system is particularly notable.

The question of how the ancients knew or intuited these celestial phenomena and intricately tied them together remains a fascinating mystery. The interconnectedness of ancient symbolism, celestial observations, and scientific understanding is an intriguing aspect of human history and knowledge.

The hexagonal dual storm system at the north pole of Saturn, Cassini-Huygens mission 2017

The connection between the hexagon or hexagram and the term "hex" is indeed interesting. The word "hex" refers to placing a curse on a person or object, akin to the actions attributed to figures like Solomon in the context of invoking entities through magic and sorcery.

Furthermore, the cube, especially the black cube, is recognized as a Saturnian symbol. Its significance is found in various ancient religions, where it represents not only the mother goddess of the earth but also Saturn. This dual representation emphasizes the multifaceted nature of symbolism and its capacity to convey layers of meaning in different cultural and religious contexts.

The Kaaba building in Mecca housing the Kaaba stone, a meteorite from Sirius in its East corner, housed in a silver yoni. This represents Saturnian, Sirius and the Goddess worship.

The connection between symbolism and worship continues in Islam, notably with the Kaaba, a black cube building located at the center of Mecca. Within the Kaaba, in its eastern corner, is a silver

Yoni, a female reproductive symbol believed to house the seed of a meteor from Sirius. It's noteworthy that before the Kaaba became a cube, it was originally a goddess temple.

During the pilgrimage to Mecca, known as the Hajj, Muslims perform rituals that involve walking around the Kaaba seven times in a counterclockwise rotation, a practice conducted during the summer months when Sirius rises above the horizon. The act of circumambulation around the structure and the subsequent touching of the Kaaba stone holds symbolic significance and can be interpreted as a form of worship connected to Saturn, Sirius, and the Goddess. This interplay of ancient symbolism and religious practices underscores the continuity of certain motifs across different cultures and belief systems.

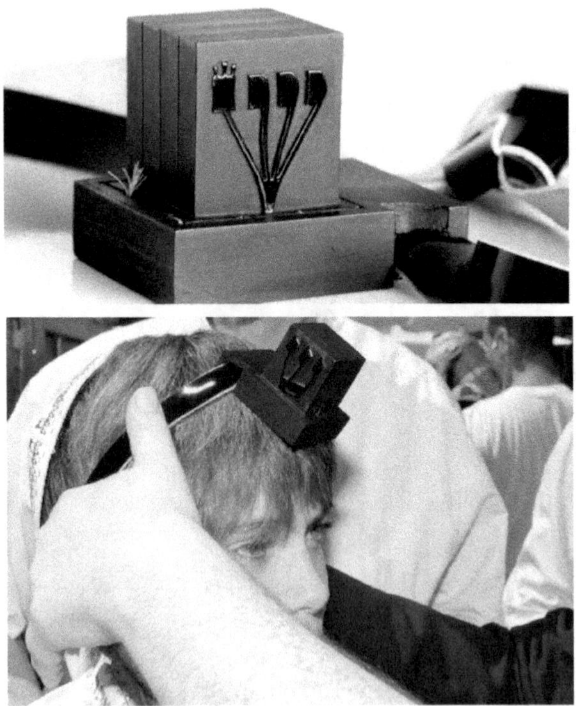

The black cube prayer box of the Talmudic Jews called the Tefillin.

In Judaism, Talmudic Jews use a black cube called Tefillin, which they wear either on their left arm or on their forehead. Tefillin houses prayers to El, a term for God, specifically referring to the Tetragrammaton or the four letters representing the name of God. Interestingly, these four letters can be represented on the four sides of a tetrahedron.

The tetrahedron, a three-dimensional shape resembling a pyramid, is one of the three magical symbols. When inverted over itself, like the configuration of the Star of David or hexagram, and counter-rotated, it forms an octahedron in the center. The hyper-dimensional or torsion field energy generated at the center of this octahedron is known as the Merkabah. The term "Merkabah" is intriguing as "Mer" means water, "ka" refers to the body, and "Ba" signifies the soul in ancient Egyptian/Khemetian or Souf language. This complex interplay of symbols and their associations can be traced back to the overarching symbolism of Saturn.

The 3-dimensional double tetrahedron of the Merkabah shape and hyper-dimensional octahedral energy.

The Brotherhood of Saturn

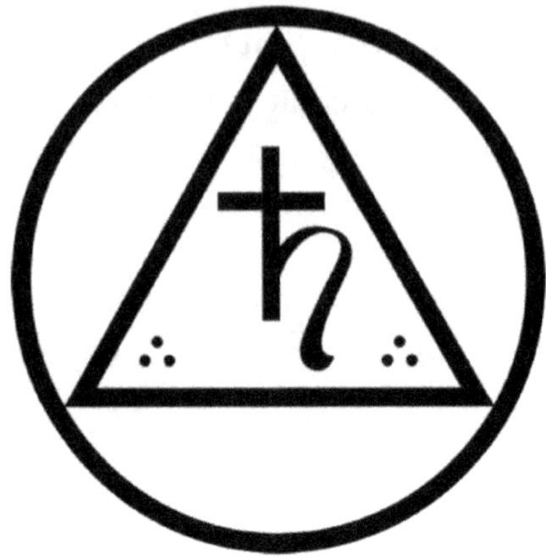

The Brotherhood of Saturn, also identified as the Fraternitas Saturni, was established in the early 20th century as a German occult and esoteric organization. Rooted in Western esotericism, it draws inspiration from various occult traditions, including Freemasonry and Thelema, placing significant emphasis on the worship and symbolism of the planet Saturn.

Key points about the Brotherhood of Saturn:

- **Founding and Influences:** Eugen Grosche, also known as Gregor A. Gregorius, founded the Brotherhood in 1928. It blends elements from diverse occult traditions, incorporating ritual magic, astrology, and mysticism.
- **Saturn Worship:** Central to the brotherhood's teachings is the worship of Saturn, symbolizing limitations, structure, and discipline. Members integrate Saturnian symbolism into their rituals and spiritual practices.
- **Magical Practices:** The brotherhood actively engages in ritual magic and ceremonial practices, prioritizing personal transformation and spiritual development. Members progress through a system of degrees, advancing through initiation stages.

- **Thelema Connections:** The Brotherhood of Saturn shares connections with Thelema, Aleister Crowley's spiritual philosophy, influencing some of its rituals and concepts.
- **Secrecy and Rituals:** Similar to many esoteric organizations, the Brotherhood maintains a level of secrecy regarding its inner workings and rituals. Members partake in ceremonies involving magical workings and initiation rites.
- **Continued Existence:** Despite challenges during the Nazi era, the Brotherhood of Saturn persevered and endures today. It has both influenced and been influenced by various occult and esoteric groups over time.

It's essential to acknowledge that the beliefs and practices within the Brotherhood of Saturn can differ among individuals and across various periods in the organization's history. Information regarding its internal workings is frequently restricted due to the emphasis on secrecy and confidentiality, a common trait among esoteric groups. Despite being banned before World War II due to the increasing German/Nazi influence in the region and era, several practices from this group influenced German/Nazi magical practices, particularly in associations like the Thule and Vril societies, where Saturn was replaced by Aldebaran.

Of note: In the new Star Wars film "The Force Awakens" (2015), the audience is introduced to the "New Order" who's symbol is a direct borrowing of the "Black Sun" symbology of the Thule Society.

The Vril Society logo next to the Thule Society logo in comparison to the First Order insignia.

Saturn Symbology in Corporate Logos

The prevalence of Saturn symbology in corporate logos related to time, travel, space, and electronics is indeed intriguing. Some notable logo examples include:

- The AAA logo
- The Dodge RAM logo, representing Moloch and the horned God of the sky
- Boeing logo
- Direct TV logo
- Internet Explorer vs. Edge logos
- Asics logo
- Nike logo
- Nintendo GameCube logo
- Sega Saturn logo
- Toyota's logo
- Saturn LLC logo
- Coca Cola and Pepsi logos
- The original NASA logo(s)
- Nissan's logo(s)
- Target logo
- The D-Wave quantum computer as a black cube
- Neutron Crypto logo
- Saturn Machine Works and even the Kronos logo.

Once you become attuned to the symbolism of the cube, bull, and other Saturnian motifs, you may indeed start to notice these patterns in various logos and symbols across different industries and domains.

The interconnectedness of such symbols and their wide-ranging appearances is a fascinating aspect of visual language and cultural iconography.

Here are some visual examples of the previous logos listed:

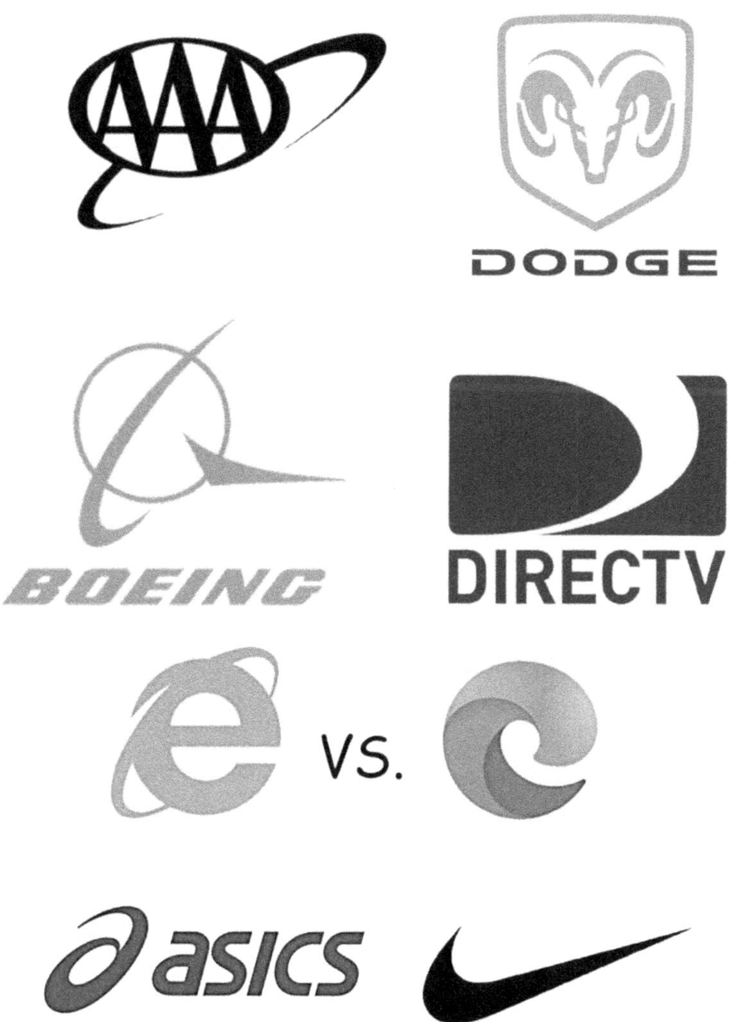

NINTENDO
GAMECUBE™

TM
SEGA
SATURN™

TOYOTA

SATURN

Coca-Cola

pepsi

NATIONAL AERONAUTICS AND SPACE ADMINISTRATION
U.S.A.

NASA

NISSAN

NISSAN

TARGET

D:wave

NEUTRON

SATURN MACHINE WORKS

KRONOS®

The movie “Interstellar” (2014) indeed incorporates significant references to Saturn. In the film, humanity faces a dust bowl or blight on Earth, prompting exploration of other planetary systems for potential relocation. The black hole featured in the movie is situated near Saturn. Notably, when the protagonist, Cooper, returns through the tesseract and black hole, Cooper Station—where the remnants of humanity reside—is depicted as orbiting around Saturn. This deliberate placement of Saturn in the movie’s narrative adds a layer of symbolism and cosmic significance to the storyline.

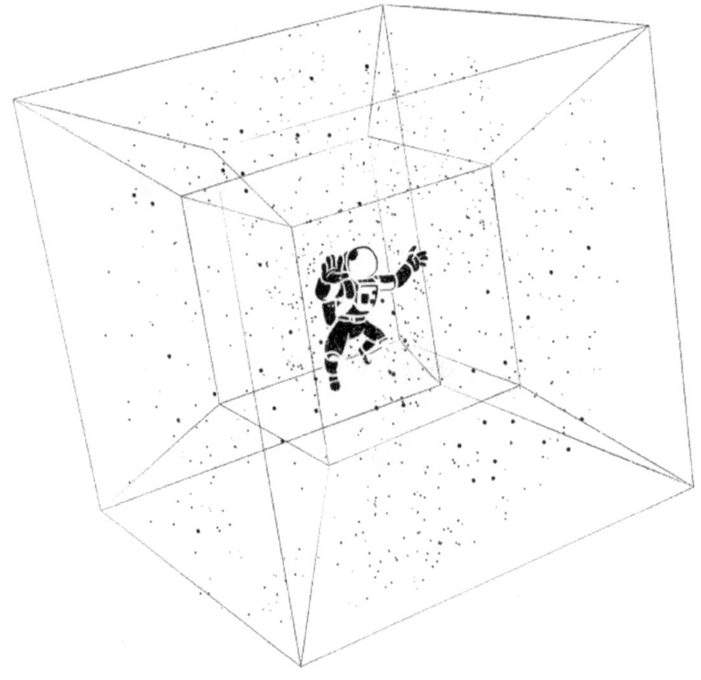

Depiction of the tesseract as a 4th dimensional cube.

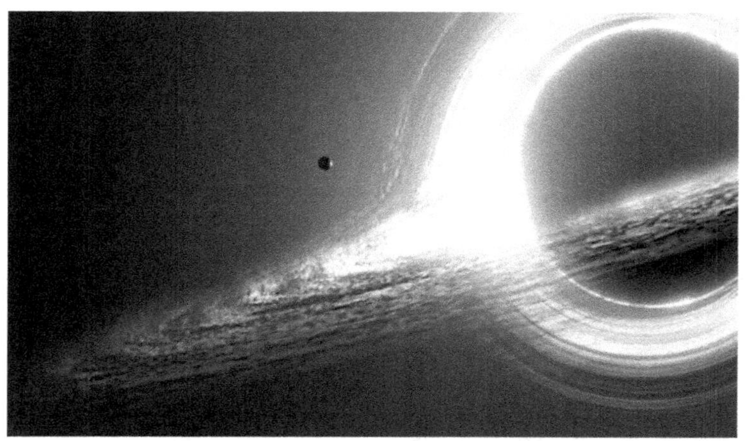

Depiction of Saturn by the very Saturn-like black hole found around Saturn's orbit in the movie Interstellar (2014).

The Saturnian object from the cover of "The Sentinel" (1951) book by AC Clarke, the origin story for "2001: A Space Odyssey" (1968).

In "2001: A Space Odyssey" (1968), adapted from Arthur C. Clarke's novel "The Sentinel" (1951), the symbolism of the cube is represented by the black monolith. In a crucial moment in the story, the monolith is discovered orbiting Saturn. The deliberate connection of the monolith to Saturn adds an additional layer of cosmic significance to the narrative, linking the mysterious object to the symbolism associated with Saturn.

Tardis (Time and Relative Dimension(s) in Space),

As Saturn, also known as Cronos, was the father of time, he would have been considered the first timelord. So, it is interesting in the TV series Dr. Who, we have the doctor, a timelord, traveling through space and time in a phone booth (the Tardis), which is somewhat a cube shape.

We have a similar reference to time travel and phone booths in the "Bill & Ted's" trilogy. In "Bill & Ted Face the Music (2020)," Saturn is portrayed as one of the planets pulled into Earth's orbit. Interestingly, Saturn is also featured on the poster of the first movie, "Bill & Ted's Excellent Adventure (1989)." And interestingly in the second installment of the movie, "Bill & Teds Bogus Journey" (1991,) Bill and Ted are palling around with Death, the Grim Reaper, which is of course a symbol of Saturn as well. The inclusion of Saturn in these three instances raises questions about its symbolic representation and the intended message for viewers. It is interesting that the world comes together through the harmonization of music.

Given the rich history of Saturn as a symbol in various cultural, religious, and esoteric contexts, its appearance in these films could carry layered meanings open to interpretation. It might symbolize cosmic forces, time, or even play into broader themes explored in the movies. The exact interpretation may depend on the specific context within each film and the director's or writer's artistic choices.

Depiction of Saturn being pulled to Earth in "Bill & Ted's Face the Music" (2020), which mimics the cover of "Bill & Ted's Excellent Adventure" (1989), and theme of death in Bill & Teds Bogus Journey (1991).

The resemblance between the Death Star in the Star Wars saga and certain features of Saturn's moons, particularly Mimas and Iapetus, is an interesting observation. The hexagonal crater on Mimas and the circular mountain structure and hexagonal craters on Iapetus do share visual similarities with the Death Star's design.

The Voyager space probes provided the first close-up images of Saturn's moons, including Mimas and Iapetus, in the early 1980s. George Lucas released the original Star Wars film in 1977, and the subsequent movies featuring the Death Star were released in the years following. It's unclear whether Lucas had specific knowledge of these moon features before Voyager's observations, but it's also possible that he drew inspiration from existing celestial imagery, scientific concepts, or even speculative ideas about extraterrestrial structures.

Lucas has cited various influences for Star Wars, including mythology, history, and science fiction, so while the resemblance is intriguing, it may or may not be a direct reference to Saturn's moons. It could be a coincidental similarity, or an artistic choice made by Lucas and the design team to create an otherworldly and visually striking space station in the Star Wars universe.

Mimas a moon of Saturn with strange hexagonal craters compared to the Death Star from the Star Wars Trilogy (1977-1984)

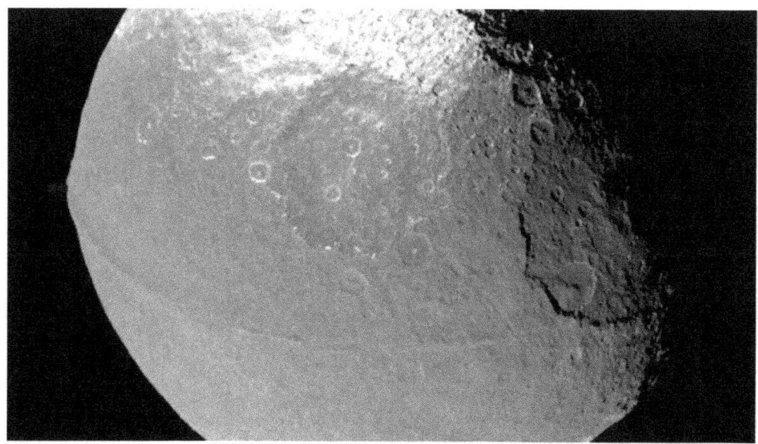

Saturn's moon Iapetus with hexagonal craters as well as a central equatorial ridge extending around the entire moon.

The inclusion of a Saturn-like planet in the Zeta II Reticuli star system in both "Alien (1979)" and "Prometheus (2017)" indeed adds an interesting layer of symbolism to these films. The nod to a Saturnian design may carry various thematic implications, especially considering the rich mythological and symbolic associations tied to Saturn.

The metaphorical theme of eating one's own children, as seen with the Aliens and Engineers in the movies, echoes the mythological narrative of Cronus (or Saturn) devouring his offspring for fear that one of them would overthrow him. This myth is woven into the narrative by director and writer Ridley Scott. The idea that man will not overthrow his maker aligns with themes of creation, rebellion, and the relationship between creators and their creations.

Ridley Scott has often incorporated complex and layered symbolism in his works, drawing on mythology, science fiction, and philosophical themes. The inclusion of Saturnian elements in these films adds depth to the storytelling and invites viewers to explore broader themes related to creation, power, and the consequences of challenging one's maker.

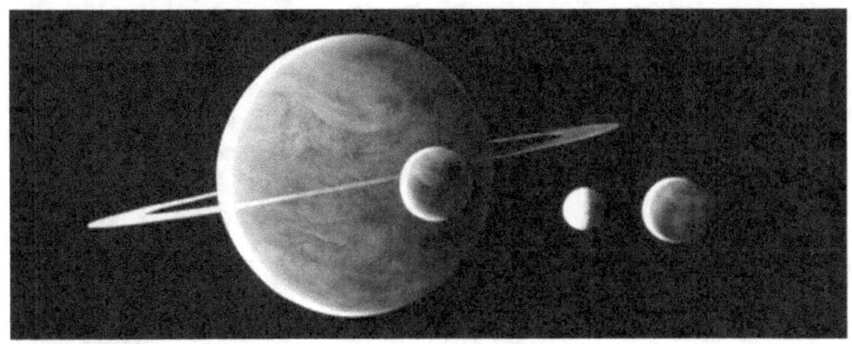

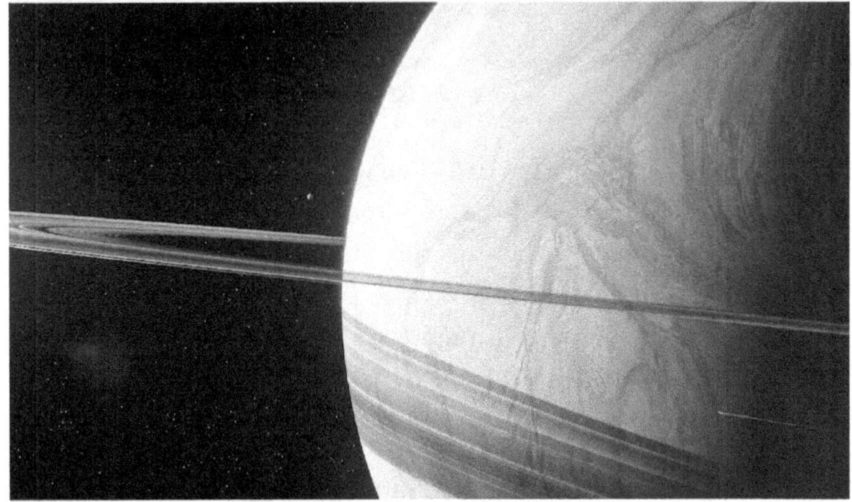

Depiction of Acheron (LV 426) from "Alien" (1979) and "Aliens" (1986), and LV 223 from "Prometheus"(2012), possibly the same Saturn-like planet with 2 different moons being used for the 2 different movies.

Another intriguing film from New Zealand is "The Quiet Earth" (1985). In this sci-fi cult classic, Zac Hobson, a mid-level scientist involved in a global energy project, awakens to a nightmare. Following a malfunction in his project, Zac realizes that he might be the last man on Earth. As he explores deserted cities in search of other survivors, Zac's mental state starts to unravel, leading to the film's iconic and widely discussed ending.

Movie poster for "The Quiet Earth" (1985) and the ending scene.

Realms of Buddhist Symbology and Sirius

In my other book, "Dropa Legends and Lore: Connecting the Ancient Secrets of Bhutan, China, Nepal, Tibet, and Sirius," I explore the rich tapestry of symbology surrounding the Stars of Sirius and Buddhist cultural mysticism. According to legend, four of the oldest and most revered relics of Buddhism originated from Sirius over 20,000 years ago. These relics were purportedly discovered atop Mt. Meru, housed within a box, and safeguarded in the clandestine city of Shambala, presided over by the Great Buddha, leader of the Great White Brotherhood.

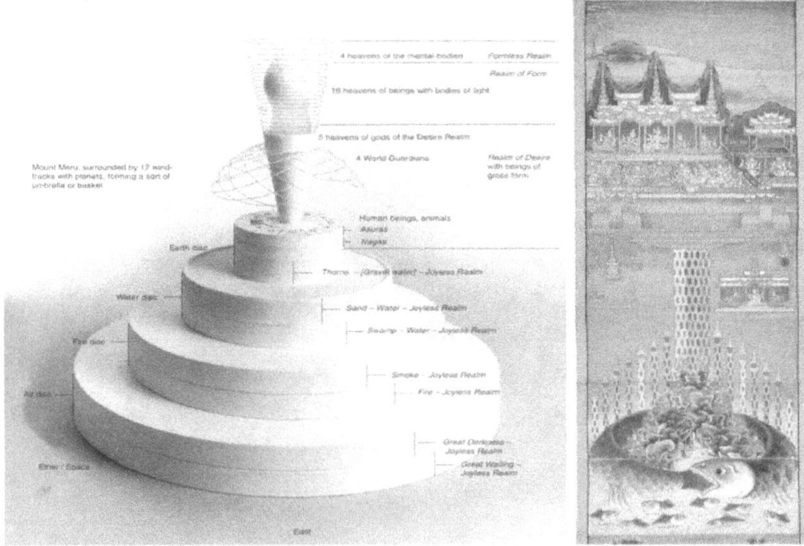

Mt. Meru, while a physical mountain located near the borders of Tibet and Ladakh, also serves as a symbolic representation of the Chakra points. In the Buddhist symbology of the mountain, each of the seven layers corresponds to vortexes of energy representing our seven levels of consciousness. These layers facilitate the transition from the lower self, or unconscious state, to the higher self, or conscious state. Within Buddhist lore, the mountain's seven layers are believed to be inhabited, with the entire structure emanating from the base chakra symbolized by the holy hidden city of Shambala (also known as Shangri-La) nestled deep within the earth. The ascent culminates at the crown chakra, representing the summit, from which energy and light extend in a rainbow-like arc towards the eastern horizon, ultimately connecting with the brilliant star of Sirius.

Recent astronomical discoveries have revealed Sirius to be a binary, and possibly even a trinary star system. Despite the profound reverence accorded to Sirius symbology, it remains one of the least understood star systems. Much of the scientific research into Sirius is conspicuously absent from public discourse or recorded history, almost as if initial investigations led to a cursory conclusion of "nothing to see here" before moving on.

The four items enclosed in the box hold profound significance within Buddhist lore:

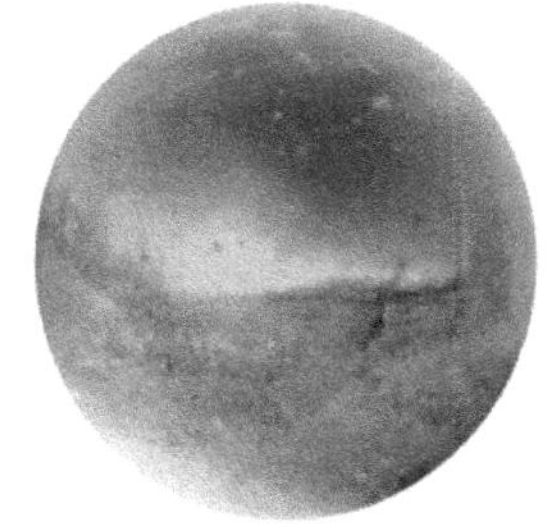

The Cintamani Stone, a celestial fragment from Sirius, is revered as the most coveted item. Believed to bestow its possessor with longevity and prosperity, it is likened to the Philosopher's Stone of alchemy. Found in diverse traditions including Christianity,

Islam, and ancient Chinese legends, it is regarded as the "luck stone" and adorned with the sacred geometry of the Flower of Life.

The Vajra Dorje, a rare four-sided lightning bolt typically crafted from Silver, Gold, or Brass, symbolizes the cardinal points of the universe. Integral to Vajrayana Buddhism, it embodies the teachings of enlightenment attainable within a single lifetime. Spiritual tools such as visualization, mantra, breathwork, and physical exercises expedite this transformative journey.

*Buddha's Singing Bow*l, when resonated by the bowl's wand, emits vibrations akin to rubbing a crystal glass filled with water. This harmonic resonance induces a healing effect and facilitates deep states of transcendental meditation, guiding practitioners towards nirvana—an enlightened state of perfect peace and happiness.

The Ohm Mani stone, adorned with the mantra "Ohm Mani Padme Hum" ("the jewel within the lotus"), aids meditators in reaching transcendental states. Repeated during deep meditation, it resonates with the singing bowl, facilitating entry into nirvana. Symbolically linked to the lotus flower, which represents the crown chakra and contains trace elements of DMT, it serves as a conduit for spiritual elevation.

Collectively, these items symbolize longevity, prosperity, guidance, and the pursuit of inner peace, with the ultimate goal of attaining enlightenment or prolonged nirvana. The journey towards becoming a bodhisattva—a being who achieves enlightenment but chooses to remain in physical form to alleviate the suffering of others—is illuminated by compassion and self-realization.

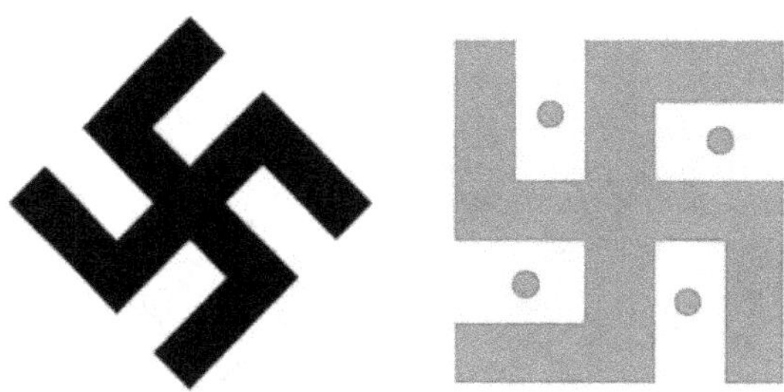

Although Buddhism boasts prominent symbols, the Swastika stands out among others due to its nearly global origins and meanings. This ancient religious and cultural emblem, depicted as a rotating armed cross in either direction, holds significance across various Eurasian, African, and American cultures. In the West, however, it is predominantly associated with the German Nazi Party, which appropriated it from Asian cultures in the early 20th century. Despite its unfortunate association, the Swastika's interpretations range from representing the occulted black sun of Saturn to symbolizing good luck and prosperity. Its widespread usage underscores its global presence and diverse connotations.

The appropriation of symbols by specific groups, such as the Nazis with the Swastika, has illuminated their true meanings and widespread historical usage. Throughout history, numerous symbols have been co-opted by cultures and religions to manipulate conquered peoples, thereby altering their original meanings significantly. This phenomenon is evident in Christianity, which incorporated elements of ancient pagan practices, transforming them into Christian holidays.

Depiction of the Swastika found around the world throughout many different cultures
Source: https://warosu.org/lit/thread/10742727 – Anonymous 2018

Likewise, in Islam, as we learned in the chapter on Saturn Symbology, the Kaaba—a black cube in Mecca originally commissioned as a goddess temple by the Queen of Sheba—underwent a transformation into a central Islamic pilgrimage site. Housing the Kaaba Stone, believed to be a fragment of a meteor from Sirius, the structure symbolizes a celestial connection. Positioned in the eastern corner where Sirius rises during the Hajj pilgrimage at the end of July, it is encased within a silver Yoni, symbolizing the feminine womb giving birth to the celestial object at the goddess temple. However, for many, these deeper symbolisms of the Kaaba and Mecca often go unrecognized.

In summary, the appropriation and reinterpretation of symbols throughout history highlight the complex interplay between cultures, religions, and the evolution of human societies, emphasizing the importance of understanding the multifaceted meanings behind these symbols.

The Mandala stands as another profound symbol in Buddhism, characterized by its intricate series of layered circles and geometries. Often associated with deities, life practices, heavens, and hells, the Mandala represents the universe in its ideal form. Its creation signifies the transformative journey from a universe of suffering to one of joy, reflecting the Buddhist principle of enlightenment and liberation from suffering.

Moreover, the Mandala serves as a powerful aid to meditation, guiding practitioners towards the realization of the perfect self. Through its intricate patterns and symbolism, it helps meditators envision the path to enlightenment and inner peace.

Two notable examples of Mandalas in Buddhism are the Kālacakra and the Bhavacakra.

Depiction of one of many Kālacakra Buddhist Mandalas (artist & date unknown)

Kālacakra: This term, rooted in Vajrayana Buddhism, embodies multiple meanings, including "wheel of time" or "time cycles." The Kālacakra Mandala represents the dynamic interplay of time, space, and consciousness. It offers practitioners a profound understanding of the cyclical nature of existence and the potential for spiritual transformation within each cycle.

Depiction of one of many Bhavacakra Buddhist Mandalas (artist & date unknown)

Bhavacakra: Also known as the wheel of life, the Bhavacakra is a visual teaching aid that symbolically represents saṃsāra, the cycle of birth, death, and rebirth. Depicted as a complex wheel with various realms and realms of existence, it illustrates the endless cycle of suffering perpetuated by attachment, ignorance, and desire. The Bhavacakra serves as a powerful reminder of the impermanent and interconnected nature of existence, urging practitioners to transcend the cycle of suffering through wisdom and compassion.

In essence, the Mandala, with its intricate design and profound symbolism, serves as a potent tool for spiritual growth and enlightenment in Buddhism. Through contemplation and meditation on Mandalas like the Kālacakra and Bhavacakra, practitioners gain insights into the nature of reality and the path to liberation from suffering.

Other notable Buddhist symbols come from some of the earliest Buddhist sites and have meaning and representation around the story of Siddhartha (Sakyamuni). Although in the west we are told that Sakyamuni was the first Buddha, it is more actual that he was considered the 1000th reincarnate of the Great Buddha who resides in Shambala and is the protector of the symbology and practices of Buddhism.

Buddhist visual art has developed an intricate vocabulary of symbolic and iconic expressions, particularly as the creation of human images of the Buddha, akin to those in Islam, was long deemed sacrilegious. Temples and Buddhist literature abound with a rich variety of symbols, among which the following eight figures are prominent:

The Lotus Flower (Padma): Symbolizing purity, wisdom (blue lotus), spiritual perfection (white lotus), and the heart (red lotus).

The Dharmachakra: The wheel of the law, with eight spokes representing the eightfold path.

The Stupa: A symbolic grave or tomb monument housing relics or ashes of holy monks, also symbolizing the universe.

The Triratna: Depicting the three jewels—Buddha, Dharma (universal law), and Sangha (community of practitioners), representing the Cintimani stone and its powers.

The Chattra: A parasol symbolizing protection from all evil, as well as a representation of dignity. It is also found in Jain and Hindu practices and beliefs.

The Dhvaja: A religious banner symbolizing the victory of Buddha's teachings.

The Deer: Symbolic of Buddha's first sermon held in the deer park of Benares (Varanasi).

The Naga: A snake deity or king, vestige of pre-Buddhist fertility rituals and protector of Buddha and Dharma.

Mudras, hand gestures, also play a significant role:

Bhumisparsa Mudra: Touching the earth to invoke witness to truth.

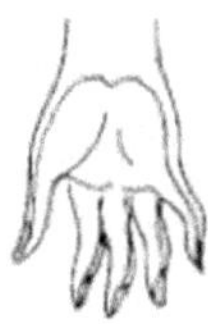

Varada Mudra: Gesture of charity and fulfillment of wishes.

Dhyana Mudra: Signifying absolute balance and meditation.

Abhaya Mudra: Gesture of reassurance, blessing, and protection.

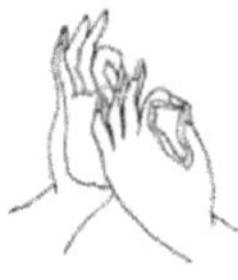

Dharmachakra Mudra: Gesture of teaching, interpreted as turning the Wheel of Law.

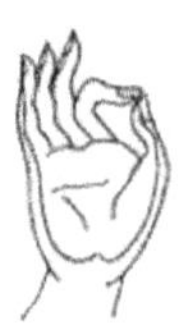

Vitarka Mudra: Signifying intellectual argument or discussion.

Tarjani Mudra: Gesture of threat or warning, usually pointed in the air or at someone or something.

Namaskara Mudra: Gesture of greeting, prayer, and adoration (also known as Namaste).

Jnana Mudra: Symbolizing teaching and wisdom.

Karana Mudra: Gesture for expelling demons.

Ksepana Mudra: Symbolizing the sprinkling of the nectar of immortality.

Uttarabodhi Mudra: Gesture of supreme enlightenment.

Images of the Buddha, crafted from the fifth century onwards, reflect a sacred representation aiming to evoke an aura of equanimity, perfection, and holiness. The meticulous execution of these portrayals requires an erudite understanding of Buddhist symbolism. Skilled artists imbue Buddha figures with multiple characteristics, communicating subtle meanings and intentions to viewers. Mudras, with fixed meanings across styles and periods, serve as essential components of Buddha images, inviting contemplation and reflection on the profound teachings encapsulated within Buddhist symbolism.

The Ampersand and the Asterisk Symbology

The ampersand, a symbol with rich linguistic and historical roots, reflects the diverse evolution of the English language. English, as a composite of various languages aiming for a universal foundation, incorporates words from diverse linguistic origins. An illustrative example is the ancient Souf/Khemetian word "Oon," which referred to the third phase of the sun, known as the "wise" sun. This term has transformed into our contemporary words "noon" and "afternoon." Notably, "Oon" was initially the name for the sun city of Heliopolis, represented by a circle with a circular dot in the center, later renamed by the Greeks.

Depiction of the eye of Ra and of Horus and the Khemetian/Egyptian symbol for the sun.

The symbolism of Horus, embodied by the eye of Horus or the eye of Ra, extends beyond the intense adolescent sun. This representation contributes to the words "horizon" and "hour(s)." Ra is also where the word "radius" comes from meaning the divine sun, or even the God Sun, but is now a measurement in geometry extending from a central point of a circle to the edge.

The ampersand, intriguingly, serves a dual purpose as both a word and a logogram, signifying the conjunction "and." Its roots can be traced to the Latin word "et," meaning "and." In certain typefaces, the ampersand visually embodies a fusion of the Latin letters E and T, showcasing the symbol's evolution and connection to the development of written language over time.

The asterisk is a versatile and intriguing symbol with various applications in writing and computer science. In appearance, it resembles a six-pointed star and is commonly employed to draw attention to specific points or information. One of its primary uses is to call out footnotes in written text. Additionally, the asterisk is frequently utilized to censor offensive words, serving as a substitute character to mask explicit language.

In the realm of computer science, the asterisk takes on multiple roles. It is notably employed as a wildcard character, indicating a placeholder for other characters in a search or pattern-matching context. This wildcard usage allows for flexible and expansive searches. The asterisk is also employed to denote pointers, indicating memory addresses, and is associated with repetition, multiplication, or as a shorthand for exponentiation in certain programming languages.

The historical roots of the asterisk are intriguing. Its design, resembling a six-pointed star, can be traced back to the symbolic joining of two arrows, converging from multiple directions. This convergence suggests a central focus or attention, which aligns with the asterisk's role in emphasizing specific content or drawing notice to particular elements within text. Overall, the asterisk's rich history and varied applications showcase its adaptability as a symbol in both linguistic and technical contexts.

Wordmarks and Spell Symbology and the Color Theory of Emotions

The use of spells or spelling is notorious in the English language, as this language was designed by John Dee and Sr. Francis Bacon (possibly two people who made up who we know of as Shakespeare). This language was developed as the common or basic tongue for the world so it would only make sense that modern spell casting is trapped in the English language, however not all spells, wordmarks or meaning is put into the English language as we see use of Latin, Germanic and other languages being used in logos that also have specific meaning. Often we will see spells expressed through the word play of corporate logos, with either words within words or wordmarks within words.

One such example of this is the logo for FedEx. This is of course a shortening of the words Federal Express indicating a fast, government service for, in this case, mail and package delivery, amongst other things. The logo itself is quite plain, but hidden between the E and the x, in the negative space is an arrow pointing forward to signify movement and express services.

Another wordmark that has an altered meaning is that for the company and thus product Spandex. Although this word does not mean anything at first glance, you can notice it is an anagram for Expands, something that the product does.

Evian is another such company, with a wordmark that really means nothing, unless one can see it as an anagram of Naive, meaning "to show a lack of experience, wisdom, or judgment"—making the slogan "Live young" meaningless and pandering to a paying audience.

Arco gas can also be seen as a spell on words as well as a sun symbol or a "spark of Archonic energy as Arco is one letter short of Arcon and a transliteration of Archon. Archon is a Greek word that means "ruler", frequently used as the title of a specific public office, but also found its way into the gnostic scriptures found at Nag Hammadi in Egypt that exposed and gave an alternative version of the biblical scriptures and thinking.

Nvidia is also an interesting logo, wordmark and thus spell, as "Invidia" is the Latin word for "envy", and it happens that this corporate logo is green, as in "green with envy", as color theory often plays into both cultural symbology and corporate symbology alike.

CISCO

The wordmark and logo for CISCO is another interesting play on both words and visuals. CISCO is obviously short for San Francisco the city of technology in Silicon Valley and the data pulse of technology, is a representation of the San Francisco bridge, while the blue color represents "the Bay", water and technology.

NOKIA

Last but not least is the logo and wordmark for Nokia. Though thought be directly related to the city in Finland called Nokia which means in older Finnish language "sable" and thus is the city's coat of arms, as a telecommunication company I feel this is a play on the word Enochian, which comes from the writing of John Dee and refers to a language of light received from the angels, much like the magic of a voice coming through a piece of technology or a Nokia phone.

Color Theory as Symbology

Poster for "Megami-ryou no Ryoubo-kun (Mother of the Goddess)" (2017-2022), depicting multiple different hair colors and thus archetypes of characters.

Other than word spells or wordmarks having hidden meaning, we also can look at color theory of logos and colors in general as symbolic representations of emotions. This is often seen in Japanamae and Manga from Japan and China as each character and thus character archetype has a different hair color. Color

Theory can also be used in Corporate Logos and Word Marks if trying to evoke a company cultural emotion. Coming full circle to the earlier examples of this, we do see a lot of logos and icons symbolically using Red, Green, Blue as main colors with a pop color of White, Yellow or even Black, and now even fluorescents.

Examples of this are:

- **Red:** Passion, Love, Anger.
- **Orange:** Energy, Happiness, Vitality.
- **Yellow:** Happiness, Hope, Deceit.
- **Green:** New Beginnings, Abundance, Nature, Envy.
- **Blue:** Calm, Responsible, Sadness.
- **Purple:** Creativity, Royalty, Wealth.
- **Black:** Mystery, Elegance, Evil.
- **Gray:** Moody, Conservative, Formality.

Applying color theory to elicit an emotional response establishes a enchanting connection to symbols through the medium of color and, consequently, emotion. The fusion of a particular color with a symbol creates a profound link, and each encounter with this color-symbol pairing subconsciously activates the associated emotion, imbuing these symbols with persuasive potency.

In essence, the deliberate use of color in conjunction with symbols creates a form of visual language that speaks directly to our emotions. This interplay cultivates a psychological response, ensuring that the recurrence of specific color-symbol combinations consistently evokes the intended emotional experience, thereby reinforcing the persuasive impact of these symbols in our perception.

Sator's Square and the Symbology of Tenet

It seems fitting to return to ancient symbology and also to discuss Sator's square in conclusion to this introduction to symbology.

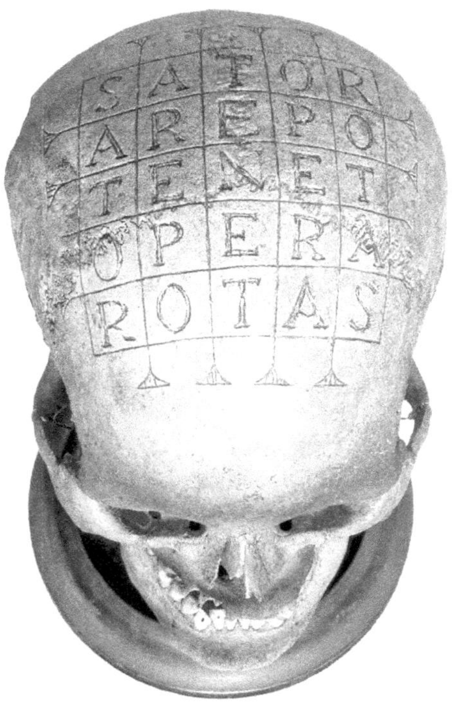

SATOR's square depicted on the 16th century Oath Skull.
A strange palindrome image from a much earlier time of spells, prayer and confessions

Sator's Square, an ancient and enigmatic arrangement of Latin words, carries profound symbolism that has intrigued scholars, mystics, and seekers of wisdom for centuries. This palindromic square, featuring the words SATOR, AREPO, TENET, OPERA, and ROTAS, forms a labyrinth of meaning that transcends linguistic boundaries and delves into the realms of symbolism and mysticism.

At its core, Sator's Square embodies the themes of symmetry, balance, and cyclical nature. The square's palindromic structure, where the words read the same horizontally and vertically, reflects the concept of eternal recurrence and the cyclical nature of existence. It suggests that life, like the square itself, unfolds in a perpetual loop, where beginnings and endings blur into a seamless continuum.

Each word within the square carries its own symbolic significance, contributing to the rich tapestry of meaning woven by Sator's Square:

SATOR: Often interpreted as "sower" or "creator," SATOR represents the divine force or the prime mover, initiating the cycle of creation and destruction. It symbolizes the origin and source of all existence.

AREPO: This word, whose meaning remains elusive and subject to interpretation, has sparked speculation and debate among scholars. Some suggest that it could be a proper name, an acronym, or a cipher with hidden meanings, adding layers of mystery to the square.

TENET: Meaning "he holds" or "he keeps," TENET embodies the concept of preservation and continuity. It signifies the inherent stability and persistence that underlies the ever-changing flux of existence.

OPERA: Translating to "work" or "effort," OPERA symbolizes the active principle of creation and manifestation. It represents the transformative power of action and intention, shaping the unfolding of life's myriad possibilities.

ROTAS: Derived from the Latin word "rota," meaning "wheel" or "circle," ROTAS embodies the cyclical nature of time and existence. It suggests the perpetual motion and evolution inherent in the cosmic wheel of life, where endings give rise to new beginnings in an eternal cycle of renewal.

Beyond its linguistic and symbolic significance, Sator's Square has also been associated with esoteric traditions, magical practices, and religious symbolism throughout history. Its presence in archaeological sites, medieval manuscripts, and occult texts attests to its enduring allure and enigmatic nature.

In essence, Sator's Square serves as a timeless symbol of cosmic order, divine creation, and the eternal dance of existence. Its labyrinthine depths invite contemplation and reflection, beckoning seekers to unravel its mysteries and glimpse the underlying harmony that binds the universe together in a symphony of cosmic proportions.

In the cryptic realms of ancient lore, where whispers of mystery intertwine with the fabric of time, one encounters the enigmatic SATOR square and the haunting Oath Skulls, relics shrouded in intrigue and steeped in the shadows of history.

Let us now again unfurl the tapestry of the SATOR square, a symmetrical arrangement of five Latin words—SATOR, AREPO, TENET, OPERA, and ROTAS—forming a palindromic square that transcends epochs. Each word intersects, crafting a labyrinth of meaning that captivates seekers of arcane wisdom.

The SATOR square, a venerable palindrome, holds the essence of timelessness within its cryptic embrace. Its origin, veiled in antiquity, eludes definitive grasp, inviting speculation and reverence alike. Some whisper of its roots in Roman times, etched into the annals of Pompeii's ruins, while others trace its lineage to pre-Christian mysticism, where it might have whispered secrets to initiates in hushed sanctuaries.

Like a riddle suspended in eternity, the SATOR square invites interpretation, its words a cryptic dance between creation and reflection. Are they the echoes of an ancient incantation, weaving spells to bend fate's will? Or perhaps they form a key, unlocking the gates to dimensions beyond mortal comprehension?

In the shadowy corridors where whispers linger, one may also encounter the Oath Skulls, relics imbued with the weight of solemn vows and silent oaths. These macabre artifacts, fashioned from bone and bound by ancient rites, bear witness to promises sworn in blood and shadows.

The Oath Skulls, guardians of secrets veiled in darkness, stand as sentinels against the tides of forgetfulness. Each skull, a vessel of memory and testament, cradles the echoes of oaths sworn in the dead of night, binding souls to ancient pacts forged in the crucible of time.

Legends weave tales of knights and sorcerers, kings and outcasts, who pledged their fates upon the brow of the Oath Skulls, their whispered promises echoing through the corridors of eternity. Some say the skulls hold the power to bind souls to their word, ensnaring the unwary in webs of obligation that stretch across the ages.

Yet, amid the whispers of antiquity and the shadows of forgotten realms, one truth remains immutable—the SATOR square and the Oath Skulls stand as testaments to the enduring allure of mystery and the eternal dance between light and darkness, beckoning the intrepid seeker to unravel their secrets and awaken the echoes of time.

The convergence of Sator's Square and Christopher Nolan's cinematic masterpiece "Tenet" is a riveting exploration into the intersection of ancient mysticism and modern storytelling. Nolan, known for his penchant for intricate narratives and mind-bending concepts, draws inspiration from the enigmatic Sator's Square to weave a tapestry of time-bending intrigue in "Tenet."

Sator's Square, with its palindromic structure and cryptic Latin words, serves as a thematic undercurrent in the film, echoing the timeless and cyclical nature of the narrative. In "Tenet," time manipulation takes center stage, and the characters find themselves entangled in a web of inversion, where the past and future coalesce in a mesmerizing dance.

Much like the square's ambiguity, "Tenet" introduces a narrative that demands interpretation and decoding. The film invites the audience to unravel the temporal complexities, mirroring the way the Sator Square beckons seekers of arcane wisdom to decipher its mysterious arrangement of words.

The parallels extend to the concept of inversion in "Tenet," where time becomes a fluid entity that can be reversed and manipulated. The Sator Square, with its intricate interlocking words, reflects the interconnectedness of time's past, present, and future – a theme echoed in the film's narrative structure.

The character Andrei Sator, whose name resonates with the enigmatic square, embodies the film's exploration of destiny, free will, and the consequences of tampering with the temporal fabric. Sator's actions ripple through time, leaving an indelible mark on the characters and the unfolding events, much like the timeless nature of the Sator Square.

The convergence of Sator's Square and "Tenet" adds an extra layer of depth to the film, enhancing the mystique and symbolism embedded in Nolan's storytelling. As the characters grapple with the consequences of their choices and the intricate dance of time, the Sator Square serves as a silent witness to the echoes of destiny and the eternal interplay between order and entropy. In this cinematic odyssey, Nolan seamlessly blends the ancient mystique of the Sator Square with the cutting-edge narrative complexities of "Tenet," creating a cinematic experience that transcends the boundaries of time and narrative convention.

Conclusion

Embarking on a journey into the realm of symbols is a captivating exploration that unveils the intricate tapestry of meanings and contexts these symbols hold. Beyond their role in communication, symbols convey not only information and culture but also occasionally conceal hidden significances beneath their surface. It becomes crucial to emphasize the importance of encouraging readers to heighten their awareness of symbols in their everyday surroundings.

Observing and deciphering symbols is a valuable exercise, offering profound insights into the cultural, historical, and sometimes esoteric dimensions of a given environment. As highlighted, symbols exhibit remarkable diversity, varying from city to city, country to country, and culture to culture. This rich variation provides a unique lens through which individuals can comprehend local contexts and influences, fostering a deeper appreciation for the manifold layers of meaning embedded in the symbolism that surrounds us.

Through this exploration, one can unravel the threads of symbolism, weaving together a narrative that enhances our understanding of the richness and complexity inherent in the symbols shaping our shared experiences. I appreciate your time and interest in reading through my introductory book on logos, icons, and symbology, as well as my reflections and opinions on the esoteric and occult usage of symbology that surrounds us every day.

Throughout this book, symbology emerges as a powerful force in history, often manifesting as a collection of images narrating tales, casting protective spells, or ensnaring individuals, entities of light or darkness, as well as specific places or historical eras. We witness prayers for luck and prosperity bestowed upon the departed for their journey into the afterlife. Cities are strategically situated and designed, creating temporal and spatial protective boundaries. Structures, both exterior and interior, are embellished with precise artworks and artifacts, reinforcing hidden or esoteric influences. With the advent of modern technology, from the printing press disseminating symbols to the masses, to television, movies, and media, a plethora of symbols and their interpretations have seeped into public consciousness.

Consequently, custodians of occult, esoteric, and secretive knowledge have sought to restrict the dissemination of their guarded wisdom and symbolic associations. Nonetheless, paradoxically, some have opted to unveil their symbology to the public eye. In the Internet age, as new technological gatekeepers emerge, dictating what can be said, heard, seen, or researched, the importance of understanding symbols becomes paramount. Any divergence from their preferred narrative prompts orchestrated campaigns to distort and obfuscate the true essence of symbols, maintaining control over secret knowledge, spells, rituals, and consequently, the masses.

Thus, it is imperative to discern the significance of symbols in our surroundings. While most occurrences do not necessitate conspiracy theories, they do require historical insight into why certain symbolic references persist, long after their inception and original practices. Are benevolent and malevolent forces engaged in a clandestine struggle within our contemporary world? The religious practices worldwide, many upheld and ritualistically observed since their inception, suggest the potential existence of such forces. Could this explain the omnipresence of ancient spells, magic, and sorcery embedded within the symbolic objects, icons, and logos of today?

HD
HANS-DIETRICH
PUBLICATIONS

www.ingramcontent.com/pod-product-compliance
Lightning Source LLC
LaVergne TN
LVHW010923110826
845149LV00013B/2459